1980

CHANGING
HUMAN
SYSTEMS

Ronald G. Capelle, PhD

International Human Systems Institute
3136 Dundas Street West
Toronto, Canada

Canadian Cataloguing in Publication Data

Capelle, Ronald G., 1948-
    Changing human systems

Bibliography: p. 224
Includes index.

ISBN 0-9690171-0-3

1. Interpersonal relations.   2. Group relations
training.   3. Social psychology.   I. Title.

HM132.C34   158'.2   C79-094828-1

ISBN 0-9690171-0-3

Printed and bound in Canada

To my mother and father

ACKNOWLEDGEMENTS

Sitting down to acknowledge one's debts of gratitude is a formidable task. So many people, alive and dead, through personal encounter and through the written word, have had an impact on me, and thereby directly or indirectly contributed to the ideas and synthesis to be found in this book. It would be impossible to attempt to mention them specifically, so to those of you who have helped, thank you.

I would like to limit my specific acknowledgements to more recent times related to this book. I am particularly grateful for the many thoughtful and insightful comments provided by friends and colleagues who read earlier drafts of this book. In particular, I would like to thank Randee Allan, John Banmen, John Begg, Steve Davison, Kenneth Enns, Steve Ferris, Jim Goodale, George Harding, Dale Hill, David Jackson, Paul Nielson, Michael Purinton, Shann Purinton, Ric Reichard, Bryan Smith, and Joan Dianne Smith.

Finally, I would like to thank Barbara J. Owen for typing earlier drafts of the manuscript and Carolyne Lederer for managing the total editorial and production processes of this book.

Contents

PART TWO

CHAPTER FOUR: Intrapersonal Change 53

PART THREE

INTRODUCTION

The diagram in Figure i:1 depicts a very simple community. This community consists of two organizations and two families. The organizations each have a main person in charge, the president. There also is a vice president to whom a group of people report. Each of the two nuclear families consists of a mother, father, daughter, and son. We are going to look at this community from the point of view of one individual in it. Let us call this individual Pat Jones. Pat plays several roles. As part of a family group, Pat is a parent to two children and a spouse.

Pat Jones is also the vice president of one of the organizations. In this organization Pat is both the boss of several subordinates and the subordinate to the president of the company.

Pat Jones contacts a human systems consultant[1,2] for assistance. There are many potential problem areas that may be causing Pat concern. The first potential problem is at the intrapersonal level in terms of how Pat deals with personal feelings and how Pat organizes time on a daily basis. The second potential problem is at the interpersonal level: two possibilities are (a) Pat Jones and Pat's spouse are not getting along well (there is a marital interpersonal problem) or, (b) there is conflict between Pat Jones and the boss (there is a boss-subordinate interpersonal problem). The third potential problem is at a group level. One possibility is that Pat Jones is experiencing family problems. For example, one of the children has recently been in trouble with the police and the counselor has said that the child's behavior is related to general family relationships and tensions. Another group problem Pat Jones could be involved in is with the workteam at the office. Perhaps this group is not getting along well. There is some dissension and subordinates don't like Pat. It

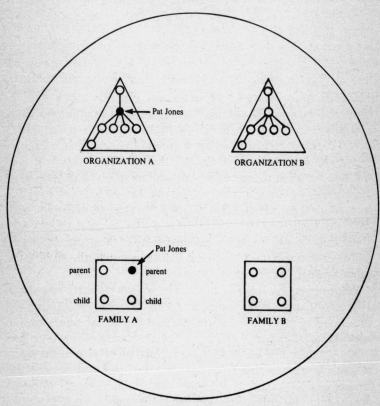

FIGURE i-1 **A hypothetical community**

could be also that Pat Jones is involved in some problems at the intergroup level. There are two possibilities: one is that Pat's family may not be getting along well with the neighbors; another is that Pat's organizational team may not be getting along with another department within the organization. The next human systems level, organization, may also be presenting problems. This little organization has recently had a consultant's report indicating that morale is low, pay isn't equitable, working conditions are poor and there is some sabotage on the production line. Next, Pat Jones may be involved in an interorganizational conflict. Pat's organization may be involved in a dysfunctional competition with the other organization in the community for scarce resources. Finally, Pat Jones may be involved, personally, in a community problem. Pat may live in a community that lacks natural resources, is unable to attract industry, and has high unemployment and political unrest.

So, with this very simple example, we have hypothetically shown that it is possible for Pat Jones to have problems at seven different human systems levels. These are: intrapersonal, interpersonal, group, intergroup, organization, interorganization, and community. Furthermore it is quite likely that the problems experienced at one level are somehow related to problems at other levels. For instance, Pat Jones' marital problems may be contributing to both the family problems and the problems with the work group; or, an interpersonal conflict with a manager in the organization may be contributing to the conflict between the organization's departments; or, the problems at an organizational level (lack of clarity of roles and responsibilities) have contributed to intrapersonal problems (feelings of insecurity), interpersonal conflict (conflict over each other's responsibilities), and group problems (lack of cohesion and low productivity). The examples of possible interrelationships between problems at the various human systems levels could be cited endlessly. The important points are that problems do occur at various human systems levels and various human systems levels are interconnected.

How would you handle Pat Jones' problems? Do you have a model for understanding how these seven human systems levels function? Do you have a model for understanding how the seven human systems levels change? Do you have a model for understanding the role of the human systems consultant in the change process at the seven human systems levels? Do you understand the similarities and differences in assessing and changing the seven human systems levels? Do you have a model for understanding at which human systems levels to intervene when it is possible to intervene at several different levels?

If the answer to any of these questions is 'no,' read on. You won't find all the answers, but you should get three things out of this book. First, you will find some useful models that I have developed to assist me in my practice. As with any models, mine are not perfect representations of the real world, and you may wish to modify them to fit more closely your particular situation. I would welcome that, and encourage you to work also at integrating these models with the other theories and models you use.

Second, you will find in this book some experiences and observations from my practice which, hopefully, will demonstrate some of the specifics of human systems consulting.

Third, as well as learning from the models and experiences, I hope you will obtain a broader perspective on human systems change. Human systems consultants, through both training and experience, tend to operate in restricted ways, missing opportunities for both more effective interventions and personal development. I do not mean to imply that all human systems consultants should be able to intervene at all seven levels. However, even the increased ability to conceptualize and recognize problems at various systems levels will increase effectiveness regardless of whether we intervene directly or bring in other resources as required.

So much for what I hope you will obtain from this book. The book itself is divided into three parts. Part One provides basic background models which are important to human systems consultants. There are three chapters in Part One. Chapter One provides a four-part model to help understand the functioning of human systems. Chapter Two provides a model of how human systems change. Chapter Three describes the role of the consultant in the change process. Both the human systems functioning model from Chapter One and the human systems change model from Chapter Two are expanded to indicate how the consultant directly influences both human systems functioning and change.

The development of these general models is an important first step for a consultant. However, it is then necessary to specifically apply the models to each of the seven human systems levels, and to recognize the similarities and differences among the seven levels. This is accomplished in Part Two, which includes seven chapters, one for each of the seven systems levels. Each chapter includes specific issues and problems in applying the models, and contains examples from my practice.

Part Three of the book contains only one chapter. It deals with the integration of the models and considers alternate levels of intervention.

Each chapter of the book except the last is followed by notes, questions, and an annotated bibliography,[3] to stimulate further thought and reading. It is certainly not my belief that one book could provide all the answers. This book is an attempt to provide some models and case material through which the reader will develop a clearer perspective on changing human systems, and also to open the doors to further reading and development.

NOTES

1. A *human system* is defined as any system involving people. For the purposes of this book seven levels of human systems will be considered: intrapersonal; interpersonal; group; intergroup; organization; interorganization; and, community. Nations and international relations could be considered higher levels of human systems but their discussion is beyond the scope of of this book.
2. A *human systems consultant* is defined as any individual who assists a human system to develop toward increased effectiveness, both in terms of the internal functioning of the system and its relationship to its environment. Human systems consultants include psychiatrists, psychologists, social workers, marriage counselors, family therapists, clergy, management consultants, staff-training and development specialists, organization development specialists and, community development specialists. As well, other members of our society may perform this role including parents, teachers, managers, and supervisors in organizations. For the sake of simplicity the term *consultant* will be used throughout the text to refer to human systems consultants.
3. It should be noted that in covering as wide an area as this book does, it is not possible to include all relevant readings. The inclusion of a book in the annotated bibliography means that I recommend it as useful further reading; the exclusion of a book does not necessarily mean that I don't recommend it.

PART ONE

Part One provides basic background models that are important to consultants. These models are presented in three chapters. Chapter One provides a four-part model to help understand the functioning of human systems. Chapter Two provides a model of how human systems change. Chapter Three describes the role of the consultant in the change process. Both the human systems functioning model from Chapter One and the human systems change model from Chapter Two are expanded in Chapter Three to indicate how the consultant directly influences both human systems functioning and change.

How human systems function

The initial task of a consultant is to be able to understand how human systems function. One of the difficulties of this task is being able to determine what aspects of human systems to consider. Figure 1:1 shows a model I have developed to assist in this understanding.

The model contains four parts. The first part involves determining what level of human system is being considered. Seven levels of human systems are considered in this book: intrapersonal; interpersonal; group; intergroup; organization; interorganization; and, community.

The second part of the model involves analyzing human systems on six basic systems concepts. These concepts include: inputs into the system; the throughput function of the system; the output of the system; feedback to the system; the boundary separating the system from its environment; and, the environment itself.

The third part of the model involves determining the developmental stage of the human system.

The fourth part of the model involves assessing eight factors that affect the effectiveness of human systems functioning. These include: objectives; structure; roles; communication; reward system; power; time; and, space.

Systems levels

Seven levels of human systems are considered in this book. These are: the intrapersonal (a single human being); interpersonal (the relationship between two people such as a married couple, or a boss

2

1) Systems level:

    a) intrapersonal
    b) interpersonal
    c) group
    d) intergroup
    e) organization
    f) interorganization
    g) community

2) Systems analysis:

    a) input
    b) throughput
    c) output
    d) feedback
    e) boundary
    f) environment

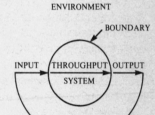

3) Developmental stage

4) General factors:

    a) objectives
    b) structure
    c) roles
    d) communication
    e) reward system
    f) power
    g) time
    h) space

FIGURE 1:1 Human systems functioning

and a subordinate); group (defined here as more than two people, which includes families and organizational work groups); intergroup (the relationship between two groups such as two families or two work groups); organization (people forming together to provide services or products); interorganization (the relationship between two organizations which have some contact); and community (a grouping, usually geographically determined, of individuals, families, and organizations).

The first step in analyzing a system is to determine which systems level is to be considered. This is usually determined by the purpose of a study or intervention. For instance, in considering our previous example of Pat Jones, if we determined that the system we were to study was the family (the husband, the wife, their son and daughter) then all other aspects (the other family and the two organizations) would be considered as part of the environment of the family. If, on the other hand, we were most interested in Pat Jones' organization, we could consider Pat's organization to be the system and all other aspects of the community, including the other organization and the two families, to be the environment. Where one draws the line between system and environment, therefore, depends on the purpose of the study or intervention being considered.

It should be noted also that a system contains subsystems. For instance, if we considered the family to be the system, then the parents would be one subsystem and the children would be a second subsystem. Similarily, if we considered the organization to be the system, then Pat Jones' work group would be one of its subsystems.

Systems analysis

The second part of understanding human systems functioning as shown in Figure 1:1 is the systems analysis. This involves six factors: input; throughput; output; feedback; boundary; and, environment. At this point we shall simply consider general examples of these factors. Later, in Part Two, we shall consider specific examples of each of these factors for each of the systems levels.

Input can range from individual input of food, water, and sensory stimulation to organizational input of manpower, money, and material. All human systems have a throughput function in which they process the input. These throughput functions range from individual throughput of digesting food and thinking about ideas to organizational throughput of transforming timber into paper or rubber into tires. Then, there are the output functions. These vary from individual output of waste excretions, opening a door and talking, to organizational output of products, services, and pollution. Next there is the feedback loop, which implies that human systems receive feedback that can be used for self-regulation. This feedback varies from our middle ear signalling us that we are about to fall, to the organizational feedback of a 50 per cent drop in sales. The next factor is the boundary around the system. This varies from the skin of an individual to the physical or membership barriers set up by an organization. Finally, we consider the environment, which contains all aspects not included in the system. Important environment aspects range from an individual's loved ones to an organization's clients.

What are the implications of this systems analysis? What are some of the more specific factors to consider? In the first place, when the system and environment are defined, attempts should be made to gather relevant information about each. What are the parts of the system? How do they interrelate? What are the relevant parts of the environment? How do they interrelate to the system?

In terms of system's input one should ask whether the human system is receiving the input it needs. This input may vary from an individual's need of food, love and affection to an organization's need of raw materials and competent staff. In terms of throughput, all systems must perform certain operations in order to survive. One should determine whether these activities are appropriate ones for the particular human system and whether these activities are being adequately performed. In terms of output, the critical question is whether the products or behaviors of the human system are appropriate for the particular situation or environment in which they exist. At an individual level the behavior should be appropriate for the situation; at an organizational level the output or products should meet environmental needs in relation to both quality and quantity requirements.

The concept of feedback is also important. Feedback is of two types: positive feedback, which maintains a system on its present course, and negative feedback, which corrects and assists a system in making changes. All human systems need an appropriate balance of positive and negative feedback. Many human systems problems relate to a lack of feedback, poor quality feedback, or feedback that is blocked out. Positive feedback is required to maintain and reinforce desirable behaviors, while negative feedback is required to change or modify negative behaviors. At an individual level, for example, children need both praise, to develop self-confidence, and also negative feedback, to establish appropriate limits of behavior. In organizations, the marketplace provides very important feedback. Positive feedback in the form of increased sales will serve to maintain and perhaps enhance production efforts; on the other hand, negative feedback, in the form of suddenly decreased sales, will often result in a significant shift in strategy with resulting behavior change. One should determine the quantity, quality and type (positive or negative) of feedback the system requires and receives as well as the system's ability to integrate and utilize it.

Next, consider the firmness of the boundary between the system and its environment. A rigid boundary will prevent the necessary exchange between the system and its environment. A loose boundary may cause the system to be flooded from the outside and lose its identity as a system. For instance, at an individual level, a person may be either too closed and rigid or too loose and lacking in self-direction. Couples experience this dilemma in a marital relationship: how to become close enough to enjoy the fruits of intimacy without losing one's identity.

The last systems analysis factor is environment, which should be considered in terms of the demands it places on the system. How well does the human system deal with environment in terms of coping with demands and pressures? How well does the system manage or influence the environment to shape some of these demands and pressures? Behavior of human systems in relation to the environment can range from dysfunctional (an individual unable to function in society or an organization producing products unwanted by the marketplace) to highly functional (an individual or organization both successfully responding to the demands of the environment while also influencing its demands).

One final point has important implications. The system, its subsystems and the environment are interdependent. This means that changes in one are likely to affect another, and necessitates careful study of the three levels to more clearly understand the interaction. Failure to do so can often lead to unexpected results. For instance, attempted changes often fail because of unexpected pressures from outside the client system. There are countless examples of this phenomenon, including the alcoholic whose spouse has a vested interest in change not occurring, or the manager returning from a training course whose organization has a vested interest in change not occurring.

Another implication of the interdependence of systems is that the causes of problems, and therefore their solutions, are not simple causal relationships (A causes B). There are usually many factors that precipitate and maintain a problem. For instance, it is unacceptable to conclude that a child's misbehavior is simply because he or she is a 'bad child.' While factors within the child (genetic or biochemical factors) may partially account for the behavior, there are usually other factors in the environment (parents inconsistently disciplining, encouragement by siblings, being spoiled by grandparents) which likely also contribute to the behavior. Another example would be an organization that complains about the low productivity of its staff. An easy answer is to say that the staff is lazy and not motivated. Again, while there may be some truth to this statement, it is likely that there are some factors in the environment (inequitable compensation system, poor working conditions) which have either initially contributed to the occurance of this behavior, or at least assist in maintaining it at its unacceptable level.

Developmental stage

The third step in understanding human systems functioning is to determine the developmental stage of the system. This is easier to do for some human systems, such as individuals for which there is an adequate amount of literature, than others, such as organizations for which there is a dearth of literature. The purpose of determining the developmental stage of a human system is to have an additional criterion for determining the appropriateness of the behavior of the human system. For instance, we would likely draw different conclusions about the appropriateness of a temper tantrum by a two-year-old as opposed to that of a twenty-two-year-old.

An additional task, which is important and related to the developmental stage, is determining whether or not the human system is currently going through any transitions. Transitions are significant events in the life of a human system which may or may not be indicative of moving into a new developmental stage. In individual terms, transitions would include marriage, birth, first job, and death; in organizational terms, they would include the starting-up of a business, the establishment of a new product line, or a merger or acquisition. The reason that these transition points are important is that they are often accompanied by stress, which may result in a temporary and normal (from a developmental point of view) regression in behavior. For instance, a child may regress to bedwetting upon the arrival of a new baby or upon first going to school; employee morale and productivity in an organization may drop immediately following a major corporate change. These events (bedwetting of a child; drop in employee morale and productivity) would likely cause less worry if they occurred during a stressful transition than if they occurred suddenly for unknown reasons. In fact, often attending too closely to a normal developmental behavioral regression related to a transition can make the problem worse instead of better.

General factors

The final step in understanding human systems functioning as shown in the model in Figure 1:1 is to consider eight general factors. These factors are: objectives; structure; roles; communication; reward system; power; time; and, space.

Objectives are statements of what a human system wants to do, or achieve. Most human systems do have objectives, although they are often vague and sometimes contradictory. Clear objectives are important in that they provide future direction and often provide a sense of meaning to a human system. Objectives also provide a measuring stick against which to assess progress. Objectives at an individual level may include educational or career aspirations, or even leisure time targets. Objectives at an organizational level may include sales targets, expected service levels or profit projections. The values[1] of a human system will strongly affect the objectives that are selected.

Structure relates to the diagraming of the relationship among individuals within a human system. It, therefore, does not apply at the intrapersonal level (where there is only one person). Structure is a very useful concept at the organization level, where it is represented by the organization chart. It is also used at the community level, when one is mapping out the relationships among various individuals and groups within the community.

We all fulfill various roles in the various systems of which we are a part. For instance, in the family system, men and women fulfill the roles of spouses and parents; in the organizational system they may fulfill the roles of managers (in relation to subordinates) and roles of subordinates in relation to superiors. Roles are positions in society which carry certain behavioral expectations. Roles allow some flexibility, so that two individuals could both successfully perform the same role and yet, in many instances, behave differently. Therefore, the final behavior is an interaction of the role description and the individual performing the role. Particular attention should be paid to situations in which a role is incompatible with the orientation of the individual performing it; the expectation of a role is unclear; or, various roles require mutually incompatible behavior.

Communication, which is a significant factor in the successes and failures of human systems, can be verbal (oral or written) or nonverbal (the medium is the message). It involves both content (the overt information transmitted) and process (the ways and means of transmitting the message). Communication can occur along cognitive (thinking, conceptual), affective (feeling, emotional) and behavioral (behaving, doing) channels. Finally, and this is an important point, communication, by definition, involves both a sender and a receiver of a message. A failure to communicate can result from faulty transmission (garbled message) and/or faulty reception (not listening carefully).

An important task is to look for incongruences in communication. These may include an incongruence between what was intended and what was sent, or received; an incongruence between verbal and nonverbal messages; or, an incongruence between cognitive and affective messages.

The reward system includes factors that are both positively and negatively reinforcing and are located both internally and externally to a human system. For instance, an individual may enjoy playing the piano (positive internal) and be praised for it by the teacher (positive external). On the other hand, the same individual may dislike doing homework (negative internal) and be criticized by the teacher (negative external). At an organizational level, an employee may enjoy doing a job (positive internal) but not be well paid for doing it (negative external). On the other hand, the employee may dislike having to act as foreperson in the regular's absence (negative internal) but be praised by peers for doing it (positive external). It is important to be able to assess the reward system in terms of direction (positive, negative), locus (internal, external) and importance (degree of significance to the human system).

Power[2] can be considered to be the ability of a human system to (a) maintain control of itself and not be controlled by others; and, (b) cause other systems to behave in ways that they would not otherwise have done. Power is an interactive concept (it requires one system to be powerful relative to another one). Power can be based on role legitimacy (we both agree that the sergeant can tell the private what to do); personal power (charismatic leaders); resource control (having money or land); or, knowledge or skill (consultants are often retained for these power factors). It often implies the right to reward or punish either directly ("You're fired.") or indirectly ("I have a headache tonight.").[3] A human system loses its power to the extent that a weaker system becomes less needy ("I don't need your money anymore, I'll go out and get my own job."). And finally, and this is a critical point, power may be either real (a fistfight between two people) or perceived (threatening to fight but not being prepared to follow through; claiming to know influential people without really knowing them). Often our perceived power is more important than our real power.

Time is an obvious and important concept. All human systems have a past, or history, which helps to shape present behavior. They are all living in the present and exhibit behaviors which can be assessed and changed. They also have a future, a direction in which they are moving, growing and developing.

In assessing a human system it is, therefore, important to have an awareness of the history of the system (particularly aspects relative to a presenting problem and previous attempts to solve the problem). There should be knowledge of present functioning obtained from self-reports, observation or third-party sources. As well, there should be some idea of possible future direction.

A further implication of the time dimension is quite obvious. How does the human system choose to spend time? This information can be used to corroborate data about values and role expectations. For instance, there is an incongruence when someone claims to value family life but chooses to spend very little time with the family. As well, it is becoming more and more important in our highly demanding society that time be managed effectively,[4] and be used to pursue the objectives established by the human system.

The ways in which human systems design and use space can be very revealing. This can provide information about the values of the human system, and should be assessed in terms of its appropriateness to the human systems objectives. Space affects the interactions we have (neighbors talk to each other; people at the ends of tables have eye contact; three children in a bedroom are more likely to fight) as well as our personal feelings and values (countries go to war over land).

10

NOTES

1. While *values* is not one of the eight general factors it clearly affects many of them, and is a particularly useful concept at the intrapersonal and community levels. Two excellent books on the subject are *Values and Teaching* by L.E. Raths, M. Harmin & S.B. Simon (Columbus, Ohio: Charles E. Merrill, 1966) and *Values Clarification* by S.B. Simon, L.W. Howe & H. Kirschenbaum (New York: Hart, 1972).
2. An excellent book on power, *Power the Inner Experience*, has been written by David McClelland (New York: Irvington Publishers, Inc., 1975).
3. These categories are similar to those presented in "The basis of social power" by French and Raven in *Group Dynamics Research and Theory,* 2nd ed., (D. Cartwright and A. Zandler, eds. Evanston, Ill: Row, Peterson, 1960).
4. A useful book on time management is *How to get Control of your Time and your Life* by Alan Lakein (New York: Signet, 1974).

QUESTIONS

1. Seven levels of human systems have been covered. Rank order your degree of knowledge of each of these levels. Rank order your level of skill at intervening in each of these levels.
2. A four-part model was presented in Figure 1 to be used to understand human systems functioning. What parts of the model do you find most useful? What parts of the model do you find least useful? Explain your answers.
3. Are there other factors not included in the model that you think should be added? List any and explain their relevance.
4. Using either the model in Figure 1, or your adaptation of it, assess the functioning of a human system (at any one level) with which you are familiar.

ANNOTATED BIBLIOGRAPHY

Kuhn, Alfred. *The Logic of Social Systems*. San Francisco. Jossey-Bass, 1976.
> A very thorough and complex approach to understanding human systems, human interactions and organizations. An excellent in-depth treatment.

General Systems Yearbook. Yearbook of the Society for General Systems Research.
> Over the years many of the more significant systems articles have appeared in this yearbook.

Miller, James G. "Living systems: Basic concepts." *Behavioral Science*, 1965, 10(3), 193-237.

Miller, James G. "Living systems: Structure and process." *Behavioral Science*, 1965, 10(4), 337-79.

Miller, James G. "Living systems: Cross-level hypotheses." *Behavioral Science*, 1965, 10(4), 380-411.

Miller, James G. "Living systems: The group." *Behavioral Science*, 1971, 16(4), 302-98.

Miller, James G. "Living systems: The organization." *Behavioral Science*, 1972, 17(1), 1-182.

Miller, James G. "Living systems: The society." *Behavioral Science*, 1975, 20(6), 366-535.
> An excellent series of articles taking a very detailed and comprehensive look at a broad range of human systems.

Von Bertalanffy, Ludwig. *General System Theory*. New York: George Braziller, Inc., 1968.
> A collection of the works of the "father of general system theory." Provides a solid background for the area.

CHAPTER TWO

How human systems change

In the first chapter we described a basic model relating to how human systems function. In this chapter we will develop a second model, relating to how human systems change. Both models are critical background models for a consultant.

When we examine today's society we find that there is very rapid change, much more rapid than was found in the past. We can see many examples of this change in terms of the economy, politics and the incredible increase in knowledge and available information. Concurrent change often involves many sectors (politics, economics) at varying rates (rapid technological change in computer industry compared to relatively slow technological change in the automobile industry) and sometimes in opposite directions (drops in stock market simultaneous with increase in real estate prices and gold markets).

What are the implications of this turbulent environment for human systems? One obvious answer is that human systems need to be able to change and adapt in order to survive. Basically, the question around change in human systems is not whether change takes place; it is, rather, discovering the most appropriate change directions and processes.

However, human systems are not simply reactors to a rapidly changing environment. Human systems can also take initiating stances and develop strategies to change the environment or to protect themselves from the need to change in certain directions.

Therefore, we can conclude that human systems do not remain static, and change partly to meet changing conditions in the environment and partly from a more proactive stance. If this is the case, how do human systems change? A human systems change model is presented in Figure 2:1, and it is suggested that the skills to master these steps are critical for successful change in human systems. The model involves nine steps. These are: analyze situation; assess change potential; set outcome criteria; generate alternative solutions; make decision; develop plan; implement plan; evaluate performance; and, reward performance.

Before we get into the specific steps of the model, several points should be noted. One is that change is an ongoing process. It is not a one-shot event where we sit there and say "Well, we are going to change now, so we will have our change session for this year." Change is a continuous process in which we are engaged. This model does not imply that change is only a stop and start process; change is an ongoing life-process.

The second important point is that one doesn't have to go through all the steps in the model all the time. There are some decisions that a human system makes and some changes which take place that don't require going through all nine steps. The purpose of the nine-step model is not to make life unnecessarily complicated. The point is to indicate the steps that human systems tend to go through and that we should be aware of. It is often instructive to develop an awareness of when steps are utilized and when they are omitted. One needs to be aware that there has to be a fit between the complexity of the process that is used and some type of a cost/benefit analysis. The amount of time and energy devoted to the process should be justified in terms of the benefits that are derived.

The third point is that we tend to "satisfice"[1] in our decision making rather than maximize. What this means is that we often pick out the first satisfactory alternative or solution that appears rather than trying to look for the one that may give us the maximum payoff. Sometimes in terms of a cost/benefit analysis this is an ap-

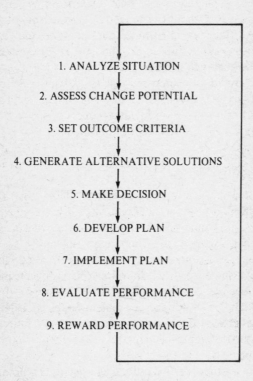

FIGURE 2:1 Human systems change process

propriate strategy, since the additional payoff may not be worth the additional effort.

The fourth and last point with regard to this model is that decisions are not totally objective, a critical point in using this model. Decision making is sometimes considered to be a purely rational process in which one obtains information, analyzes it and makes a decision. This is not true. There are other more subjective elements that come into play. At a personal level, feelings come into play. How does one feel about this person? How does one feel about this activity? At other levels attitudes may be important. At still other levels values may be important. The goal is not to eliminate these factors. The goal is to achieve a balance, to arrive at a decision that makes sense and has some rational basis, while at the same time taking into account feelings and attitudes and values. This is an important part of any decision-making process.

Let us now consider the steps of the model.

Analyze situation

The first step in the change process is to analyze the situation. The model of human systems functioning (Figure 1:1) may be useful in this process. It would lead to information on the level of human systems being considered; a human systems analysis; the developmental stage; and, consideration of the eight general factors.

It would also be important to more specifically consider any areas which are seen to be dysfunctional, or which present opportunities for growth and development. A problem can be considered to be the difference between the current situation and the desired situation.[2] If there is no difference between these two there is no need to continue the process.

Once the problems are identified and listed, two points should be considered. First, it is important to attempt to reach the underlying problem and not simply the symptoms. For instance, if a small child is acting out at home, the problem could be incorrectly defined as the child's misbehavior. This, in fact, may be simply a symptom of marital dysfunction. Another example would be the poor performance of workers in a plant. This may be only a symptom and the underlying problem may be one or more of a number of factors including poor selection, poor training, poor supervision, and/or an inadequate reward system.

The second point which must not be forgotten is that if we accept a systems perspective we must assume that problems often have multiple causation and that there is not one simple single cause. The implication of this for the change process is that often several inter-related solutions dealing with various dimensions of the problem will be more effective than a single solution.

Assess change potential

Once the situation has been analyzed and the problem areas are identified and analyzed the potential for change must be assessed. This is a critical step since without sufficient momentum and commitment, the problem may not be corrected. Unfortunately, often the only assessment of potential that takes place is a post hoc rationalization of intervention failures. There are three critical questions that should be asked relating to the system's motivation, skill and power to change.

(a) Is the system motivated to change? This is often referred to as the *felt need* of the system in organizational terms, or *pain* in psycho-therapy terms. Unless the motivation for change is fairly high, the benefits of change may not outweigh the costs of the change process and the system may prefer to remain in its present circumstances. This is particularly true if there appear to be no risks in not changing. Another way of viewing this concept is in terms of how serious the problem is to the effectiveness of the human system and how urgent it is that action be taken.

It is assumed that human systems need to be motivated in order to change. Where levels of motivation are low it is necessary that they be increased to a higher level in order to proceed with the change process. There are some ways that this can be accomplished. The first is simply making the human system more aware of the effects of the problem. There is, sometimes, a lack of awareness of the real effects of the problem and pointing out some of the negative consequences of that behavior may be useful. The second approach is to be aware of ways in which the costs or perceived costs of the change process can be decreased. The flip side of this point is that human systems can become more aware of the potential benefits. Both of these are related to the expectations of a human system in relation to the change process. These expectations often become a self-fulfilling prophecy.

The implication of this point is that it is critical for human systems to develop expectations that are realistic, attainable and meaningful. My experience has been that the most difficult situations are often either with human systems which have low expectations and never get hooked in the change process, or with human systems which have high expectations and are invariably disappointed. Therefore, working on the level of expectations can be an essential strategy.

A third approach to increasing motivation is through creating environmental pressure for change and increasing the cost of the current behavior. Examples of this would be the imposing of fines by government on business for pollution or parents taking away the allowance of a misbehaving child.

(b) A second question is whether or not the human system has the skills or abilities to change. This is a critical question since a highly motivated system without the required skills will not be successful. If the skills are not present the secondary question is whether or not the skills are trainable. This is often difficult to determine and may require special diagnostic procedures. If the skills are not present but trainable the first step of the implementation would be the training of these skills. (I can ride bike—skill present/I can't ride bike but have physical abilities to learn—skill not present but trainable/I can't ride bike and am crippled—skill not present and not trainable.)

(c) A third question is whether or not the human system does have the power to change. We all have limited power to make certain changes. For instance, children in families have little effect on a family's gross income; middle-level government managers have little effect on a government's policy. However, it is important to remember that while power is partially defined by our roles and responsibilities, it is also a personal characteristic. While there are certainly limits to power, to some extent people have as much power as they think they have. Therefore, in situations where there is a perceived lack of power it is important to sort out the personal aspect which may be utilized even in the absence of legitimate power. Where both seem to be missing, the subsequent questions would be whether those with the legitimate power could be influenced, or whether more personal power could be developed.

These three areas, motivation, skill, and power, are shown in Figure 2:2. It is assumed that in order to proceed with a change process at least medium levels of motivation, skill and power are required. If the initial assessment indicates that one or more of these areas is below the medium level it would be necessary to increase that level before beginning the change process per se.

LEVEL OF CRITERIA

	LOW	MEDIUM	HIGH
MOTIVATION			
SKILL			
POWER			

TYPE OF CRITERIA

FIGURE 2:2 Criterion grid to assess change potential

Set outcome criteria

Once the situation has been analyzed and the change potential has been assessed it is time to set outcome criteria. There are two aspects with which to be particularly concerned. One is the results or outcomes desired and the other is the resources that can be committed to the change process.

In terms of objectives or results it is important to specify results that are clear, specific, attainable, and measureable. It is also useful at this point to distinguish between results that are critical (needs which must be met) and results which are less critical (wants which are desirable but not necessary). For instance, if I go to university I may set up passing all of my courses as a need, but determine that making the Dean's Honor List is a want which is not as critical. It should also be noted in passing that the results we set have important value implications.

In terms of resources, it must be determined what resources are available to work on the change process. There are three main resources to consider: time, money, and materials. Time is the most basic and is critical to any change process. More specific questions on this dimension would be: whose time? how much of it? and, over how long a period? The second most important resource is money. Many change processes involve money, particularly if an external consultant is involved in the change process. The third resource, materials, may or may not be required. This is more important in larger projects.

Having completed the list of results and resources, it should be pointed out that the benefits derived from the results should be greater than the cost of the resources. If this is not the case it is necessary to reassess.

Generate alternative solutions

It is now time to generate alternative solutions for the identified problems. These solutions will hopefully lead to the desired results within the resource limitations. The problem with this step is that we all have our pet solutions which we nonjudiciously apply to most problems. It is important, therefore, to attempt to generate various alternatives. This can be done simply by writing down all alternatives that come to mind without censoring, and only later assessing the feasibility of the alternatives. The value of this approach is that an idea that seems not feasible and would not normally be considered may, in fact, be feasible or at the very least provide an insight that can be utilized to provide a better alternative.

Make decision

The step of making the decision, providing that the previous steps have been properly completed, is relatively simple. The criteria (results and resources) and alternative solutions (the most seemingly feasible of those generated) can be placed on a decision matrix such as shown in Figure 2:3. Each alternative solution is rated against each result (does the alternative achieve the result?) and each resource (does the alternative fall within the limitations demanded by the resource?). The rating system can be either dichotomous (a plus indicates the alternative meets the criterion; a minus indicates it does not meet the criterion) or multidimensional (rating on a scale of one to ten as to how well it meets the criterion). It then becomes a matter of adding up the ratings on the various dimensions.

However, before making a final decision, it is useful to consider any costs, risks or negative consequences for each alternative that may not have been considered up to this point in time. Having done that it is now time to make a decision, and one or more of the solutions may be chosen as being best able to solve the problem and obtain the desired results within the resource restrictions.

It must be pointed out that this step has been presented as an extremely rational step. For some types of problems this is the case. However, for other problems of a more highly charged nature (involving strong feelings or values) the decision-making step is not nearly as neat or clear.

Develop plan

Now that the solution(s) have been chosen, a plan should be developed. A plan is the link between the processes that have been completed and the action that has to be taken. The means and strategies of implementation must be considered. The basic questions are: What is going to be done? Who is going to do it? and, When will it be done?

It should be noted that planning often involves more than one step. If this is the case the linkages between the steps must be considered. More complex planning may require the use of a specialized

CRITERIA

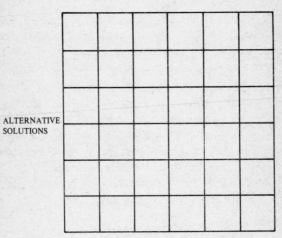

ALTERNATIVE
SOLUTIONS

FIGURE 2:3 Decision matrix

technique such as the Program Evaluation and Review Technique (PERT).[3]

It is often advisable for plans to be incremental, that is, involving small steps, rather than trying to accomplish everything at once in one or two steps. This approach increases the probability of success, particularly in the early steps which are so critical.

One aspect of planning that is critical is the development of a reward-and-support system for the planned change. While this process should be considered at the planning stage, or before, we will consider it as the final stage of the model.

Another point related to planning that is important is the recognition that the implementation of plans is rarely a smooth process. Often, the environment changes, unforseen circumstances occur or support systems realign. It is, therefore, advisable to ascertain that expectations around change are realistic. It is sometimes advisable to role-play possible difficult situations to develop pre-implementation skills.

Implement plan

The major problem in implementing a plan is that people don't recognize its inherent complexity. The implementation stage will not likely go as smoothly as planned, and will likely require some modifications to the original plan. This type of flexibility must be built into any plan. As well, support-and-reward systems must be utilized, especially when the change process experiences difficulties.

Since this stage will be considered in detail in subsequent chapters, we will not discuss it further at this time.

Evaluate performance

This step is critical in order to determine whether the change process was successful and to further determine implications for future similar projects. Evaluation may range from the very simple ("I feel good about this change.") to the very complex (a multivariate analysis involving control groups). While from a research point of view the more objective and controlled the evaluation the better, this is often not possible (or necessary) in actual change processes. However, what does seem eminently reasonable is that we become more aware of the ways in which we evaluate and ascertain that evaluations do provide the basic information that is required.[4]

Reward performance

This is the step that is often missing from the change process. The successful change process must include the development and utilization of a reward-and/or-support system to maintain the desired results once they have been initially achieved. There are countless examples of initial successes that turn into subsequent failures. At the individual level, we can look at attempts to lose weight or to stop smoking. At the organizational level, we can note attempts to implement Management by Objectives projects; in the very near future I am sure we can add programs to implement Zero-Based Budgeting to our list.

There are two aspects to be considered. At one level there should be an intrinsic value of the change to the system. For instance, the individual may feel more competent or successful, or the family may have fewer fights. At another level, though, it is often necessary to build in extrinsic motivation. For instance, in an organization, if the staff successfully undergoes a difficult change they should be rewarded in some way. Possibilities include praise, money, time off, recognition, promotion, or autonomy. But the critical question is "What is going to maintain the change once it has been accomplished?"

The final point to consider is the use of support groups. These are groups designed to support each other through the difficult parts of the change process. By acknowledging the need for and beginning the development of these groups, it is possible to minimize the possibility of the change process dying.

NOTES

1. This is a term introduced and described in *Organizations* by J. March and H. Simon (New York: Wiley, 1958).
2. This definition has been suggested in *The Rational Manager* by C.H. Kepner and B.B. Tregor (New York: McGraw Hill, 1965).
3. A very good primer on this technique is *A Programmed Introduction to PERT* by the Federal Electric Corporation (New York: Wiley, 1963).
4. A useful primer in this area is *Experimental and Quasi-Experimental Designs for Research* by D.T. Campbell and J.C. Stanley (Chicago: Rand McNally, 1963).

26

QUESTIONS

1. A nine-step change model was presented in Figure 2:1. How does this model compare with your experience of the change process? Are there parts of the model you would like to see added or deleted? Explain.
2. Analyze a situation (Step One of the model) in which you are involved using the systems concept of Chapter One.
3. Assess the change potential (Step Two of the model) in the situation you have selected. Are there any special questions or tests you can use to assist in this assessment?
4. Complete the final seven steps of the model for the situation you have selected.

ANNOTATED BIBLIOGRAPHY

Bennis, W.G. Benne, K.D. Chin, R. & Corey, K.E., eds. *The Planning of Change* 3rd ed. New York: Holt Rinehart & Winston, 1976.
The highly revised third edition (previous editions in 1961 and 1969) of an outstanding book of readings in the change area.

Hornstein, H.A., Bunker, B.B., Burke, W.W., Gindes, M. & Lewicki, R.J., eds. *Social Intervention: A behavioral science approach*. New York: The Free Press, 1971.
A good book of readings concerned with more macro approaches to change. While some of the material is now dated many other issues raised are of current significance.

Janis, I.L. & Mann, L. *Decision Making A psychological analysis of conflict, choice and commitment*. New York. The Free Press, 1977.
A truly outstanding analysis of decision making at several different systems levels. An important reference for those interested in the change process.

Lippitt, G.L. *Visualizing change: Model building and the change process*. Fairfax, Va.: NTL Learning Resources Corporation, 1973.
A valuable book not only for insights on the model-building process but also for discussion of change models at various systems levels.

Lippitt, R., Watson, J. and Westley, B. *The Dynamics of Planned Change*. New York: Harcourt, Brace & World, 1958.
One of the first important books in this area, it provides a historical perspective on the origins of much of contemporary thinking.

Watzlawick, P., Beavin, J.H., & Jackson, D.J. *Pragmatics of Human Communication*. New York: Norton, 1967.
A stimulating look at the behavioral effects of human communication. Discusses potential pathologies in human communication and develops some hypothesis about the therapeutic process.

Watzlawick, P., Weakland, J. Fisch, R. *Change: Principles of problem formation and problem resolution*. New York: Norton, 1974.
Expands on the previous work and develops some provocative ideas about the change process. Provides many examples which demonstrate that rational is not always what it appears to be. You may not agree with all of it, but it certainly provides much food for thought.

CHAPTER THREE

The role of the consultant in the change process

In the previous two chapters we discussed how human systems function and how they change. It is interesting to note that we have still not demonstrated any need for a consultant. It is quite clear that human systems can often function and change without any assistance from consultants. On the other hand we know that consultants are often retained to assist human systems to change and function more effectively. What are the reasons for retaining a consultant?

To answer the question in a very general way, a consultant can often provide the factors that may not be sufficiently present in the human system to generate a high probability of successful change. More specifically, I believe that a consultant can provide five resources to a human system: objectivity; motivation; skills; power; and, time. Let us consider each of these factors.

One of the most important factors a consultant brings to a human system client is objectivity. It is often the case that clients are so involved in the problem that they lack the necessary objectivity to effectively assess and change the problem. The client may even possess sufficient skills and motivation, but be so immersed in the problem as to be unable to see it clearly or change it. Examples of this would include competent counselors who need assistance with their own family problems, or competent managers who are immersed in organizational problems and require assistance.

While it may seem at first glance that the consultant brings objectivity by virtue of third party status, this is only part of the story. In order to effectively discharge this responsibility a consultant should possess a high degree of self-awareness to prevent personal biases from creeping into the relationship with the client. Examples include a therapist not allowing personal feelings about parents to affect consultative behavior with a client, and a management consultant not laying 'personal' values on an organizational client. The development of this self-awareness is a life-long process and is critical to successful consulting.

The second situation that would indicate the usefulness of a consultant is the client motivation to change being low (although not too low). In the first place the very act of requesting a consultant to assist with a problem often provides some motivation. As well, the presence of the consultant is often in itself a motivating factor. The basis of this is often the quality of the relationship between the consultant and the client. For instance, I have had organizational clients see me in the hall and immediately think "Oh no, I haven't completed that task yet; I'll get going on it this afternoon." There is a danger of the consultant overplaying this role and becoming the sole focus of motivation. This is certainly to be avoided; however, in moderate degrees this is a real and important contribution of the consultant.

The third factor and perhaps the most obvious, is the skills that a consultant can bring to the change process. Often the human systems client does not, in fact, have sufficient skills to bring about a change process. The deficiencies may include lack of understanding of the situation, lack of awareness of alternative solutions, or lack of skills in managing the change process. Naturally, it is the responsibility of consultants to determine whether or not they actually do possess the requisite skills. In situations where they do not possess these skills it would be important to not get into the consulting relationship and provide an appropriate referral.

The fourth factor related to bringing in a consultant is the power or leverage or credibility that a consultant can bring. A competent, respected consultant with a good reputation can provide a credibility that would otherwise not be possible. For instance, in an organization, a manager, alone, may fail to gain acceptance of a change plan, but with the additional credibility of a consultant the plan becomes accepted.

As an aside, there is an unfortunate by-product of this stance which is that often people within the organization are not listened to as carefully and frequently as they should be. The cliché comes to mind—"It is difficult to become a prophet in your own land." Consultants should, therefore, attempt to assist a client in recognizing and utilizing good internal suggestions, not always relying on external validation.

The fifth and final factor is time. This factor is more important in larger human systems such as organizations or communities. There are situations where one of these larger systems has all of the requisite objectivity, motivation, skills, and power, but lacks the necessary time to handle the change process itself. Rather than reallocating staff workloads a consultant will be called in. This is certainly a legitimate use of a consultant's services; however, it is important to determine that bringing in a consultant is not an indication of a lack of a strong organizational commitment to the change process.

While human systems often function and change without the aid of a consultant, there are times when it is appropriate to bring in a consultant. A consultant, in order to be effective, must be able to both assess the functioning of a human system and, on the basis of this assessment, facilitate a change process. Further, in order to be able to assess and facilitate change, a consultant must have appropriate models to understand both of these aspects. Two models were developed in Chapters One and Two to show how human systems function and change. However, these were basic systems models that did not take into account the presence of a consultant. Therefore, I have adapted these basic models to take into account the presence of a consultant and will spend the rest of this chapter discussing (a) the consultants' human systems assessment model; and, (b) the consultants' human systems change model.

Human systems assessment

The consultants' human systems assessment model is shown in Figure 3:1. This model will provide much of the basic information required for consultants working at any of the seven human systems levels. The model contains five areas. The first four areas (systems level, systems analysis, developmental stage, and general factors) are identical to the four factors in the human systems functioning model (Figure 1:1). These factors, and the discussion relating to them in Chapter One, remain identical with the addition of a consultant to the process. In order to assess the human system it would be necessary for the consultant to: (1) determine the appropriate systems level (intrapersonal, interpersonal, group, intergroup, organization, interorganization, and community); (2) analyze the system (including input, throughput, output, feedback, boundary, and environment); (3) determine the developmental stage; and, (4) consider general factors (including objectives, struc-

1) Systems level:

   a) intrapersonal
   b) interpersonal
   c) group
   d) intergroup
   e) organization
   f) interorganization
   g) community

2) Systems analysis:

   a) input
   b) throughput
   c) output
   d) feedback
   e) boundary
   f) environment

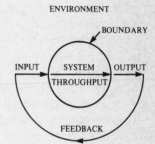

3) Developmental stage

4) General factors:

   a) objectives
   b) structure
   c) roles
   d) communication
   e) reward system
   f) power
   g) time
   h) space

5) Client-Consultant relationship

FIGURE 3:1 Consultants' human systems assessment model

ture, roles, communication, reward system, power, time, and space).

The only major difference between the original model and the adapted model is the addition to the adapted model of a fifth dimension, namely the client-consultant relationship. If we assume that a human systems client is not in isolation but is interacting with the environment, then we must assume that there is an interaction between this client and the consultant. Not only does the consultant affect the client, but in this interactive system the client also affects the consultant. Consultants often only consider the human system in isolation with a resulting lack of accuracy in assessing the system.

One of the implications is that we must diagramatically indicate the presence of the consultant. The diagram in Figure 3:2 indicates that if we initially consider a single human system to be the client (intrapersonal, group, organization, or community) we must now consider the interaction[1] between the client and consultant. It also shows that if we initially consider the relationship between two systems (interpersonal, intergroup or interorganization) to be the focus of change we must now consider the transaction[2] among the two client systems and the consultant.

Let me give you two examples to illustrate the need for this level of assessment. In doing individual psychotherapy it is quite possible for a therapist to attribute a patient's behavior solely to the patient and not consider the effects of the relationship with the therapist or the effects of the situation (therapy session in psychotherapist's office).[3] However, much of our behavior is generated as much by the situation in which we find ourselves (being in church or a baseball stadium; being with parents or a spouse) as by our personal tendencies (we have varying tendencies to express feelings). In a psychotherapy situation much of the behavior (gestalt therapy patients emote, psychoanalytic patients have psychoanalytic dreams, primal patients move toward a birth experience) is largely caused by the situation and relationship with the therapist. Unless the therapist can recognize this and sort out the factors more attributable to the person and more attributable to the relationship or situation, the error of attributing everything to the client and nothing to the interaction between them will occur.

A second example would be a consultant working with an organization. The consultant has done a thorough analysis of the organization and has begun the change process. As problems occur the consultant looks for errors in the original analysis, or blames the

34

WHEN WE ADD A CONSULTANT | ◯ CONSULTANT

TO A HUMAN SYSTEM CLIENT | ○ CLIENT

WE MUST CONSIDER THE INTERACTION
BETWEEN THE TWO IN OUR HUMAN
SYSTEMS ASSESSMENT

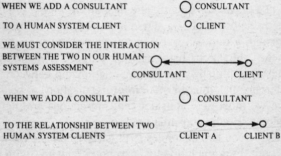

CONSULTANT   CLIENT

WHEN WE ADD A CONSULTANT | ◯ CONSULTANT

TO THE RELATIONSHIP BETWEEN TWO
HUMAN SYSTEM CLIENTS

CLIENT A   CLIENT B

WE MUST CONSIDER THE TRANSACTION BETWEEN THE THREE IN OUR
HUMAN SYSTEMS ASSESSMENT

CLIENT A   CLIENT B

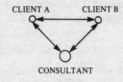

CONSULTANT

FIGURE 3:2 Diagrammatic representation of client-consultant relationship

organization for not being motivated. The consultant fails to consider the actual relationship with the organization, which may be the 'actual' cause of the problem. And, having blinders to this particular area, the consultant fails to solve the real problem.

It is, therefore, necessary for the consultant to consider the relationship with the client. The variables already presented in the consultant's human systems assessment model (Figure 3:1) could be reconsidered in terms of the client-consultant relationship. It would be useful, in most situations, for the consultant to scan over the list and determine which factors are most appropriate. In my experience, the two most critical factors generally have been communication and power.

The importance of communication in the consultant-client relationship is virtually self-evident. This is the channel through which the consultant conducts the human systems assessment and change process. It is critical for a consultant to be able to communicate effectively as well as assess a client's communication.

Power is also an important variable, particularly at the more complex human systems levels. It is important for consultants to be able to assess their own power base and determine if it is adequate for the task. This seems to be particularly important in organizational consulting where the lack of an adequate power basis is one of the main reasons for project failure.

As well, the consultant should keep two further points in mind with regard to the client-consultant relationship. The first is that the consultant serves as a model for the client, and must, therefore, be aware of personal behavior and the effect that it has upon client learning. We often like to think that clients only learn from what we tell them; however, they often learn more from observing us, and incongruities between what we say and do readily become apparent.

The other point is that the consultant can consider the relationship with the client to be a symptom of the client's other relationships. Therefore, this relationship in itself has the potential to provide useful diagnostic data. For instance, one organizational client who kept me waiting had a serious time management problem, and kept most people waiting. A counseling client was extremely nice and agreeable with me, and turned out to have a problem dealing with disagreement and conflict. However, a note of caution is necessary. Remember, you are meeting with the client in a particular situation with particular role expectations. The client may or may not transfer these behaviors into other situations. I can think of more than one client who treated me with respect and yet treated subordinates poorly.

We will conclude this section by pointing out that the purpose of the assessment model for the consultant is to provide information on human systems function and dysfunction which will lead to a change process. Throughout the assessment the consultant should be considering change processes which may help to alleviate the areas of dysfunction. While the categories of the model are not exhaustive, and while some areas of dysfunction may fall outside these categories, they are, nevertheless, a useful basic framework. This is particularly true for the systems analysis and general factors sections of the model.

The six systems analysis categories could each lead to specific interventions. Examples include: modification of input (better diet for an individual; better recruiting for an organization); throughput (reorganizing a business to cut down on redundant operations; helping an individual to decrease the frequency of obsessive thoughts); output (helping a child to decrease tantrums; helping an organization to more effectively distribute their product to clients); feedback (an individual who tends to talk too much at meetings asking for feedback from his peer group; an organization developing a better market research program to anticipate changes in client needs); boundary (helping an isolated, constricted person to socialize more; helping an organization increase company identification and decrease turnover); and environment (helping an individual to develop more awareness of people and situations; helping an organization to deal more effectively with increased government regulation).

As well, dysfunction in the eight general factors of the model can also lead to specific interventions. For instance, lack of clarity of objectives can lead to an objective clarification exercise; an inappropriate structure can lead to a reorganization; lack of role clarity can lead to a role clarification process; an inadequate information system can lead to helping an individual to listen and give feedback more effectively, or helping an organization to develop a better system of memo distribution or meetings; an ineffective reward system can lead to working with individuals to increase positive feedback or working with an organization to revise its compensation system; problems with power can lead to a power reallocation or a modification in its use; time problems can lead to developing more effective time management skills; and space problems can result in a reallocation of space.

While these examples are not exhaustive they do serve to illustrate some of the possible links between assessment and change. The assessment process must serve two functions: (a) provide a comprehensive understanding of the functioning of the human system; and, (b) serve as the basis for developing an intervention strategy and process.

Human systems change

The second model that is important for a consultant is a model of how human systems change with the assistance of a consultant. This model is shown in Figure 3:3. This model is adapted from the human systems functioning model shown in Figure 1:1. In fact, the human systems change model includes all nine steps from the previous model to which I have added four steps necessitated by the presence of a consultant. These steps are: begin relationship; assessment contract; intervention contract; and, end relationship. These four steps are shown in boxes in Figure 3:2 to indicate that they are new steps.

Before discussing these four new factors it would be useful to consider in more general terms how the presence of the consultant modifies the change process. The major difference, as indicated by the previous discussion of the client-consultant relationship, is that all steps involve both the consultant and the client, and there must be a decision as to what roles and levels of activity each will maintain.

Consultants vary in the degree of problem-solving activity and responsibility they assume. For instance, at one end of the continuum there are counselors saying that one should be process-oriented and not make decisions, and that advice (content) is not helpful.[4] At the other end of the continuum, there are counselors who say that their job is to help clients become aware of irrational processes, which contribute to bad decision making, making it often necessary to be argumentative and directive. Organizational consultants operate on a similar continuum. Some will say that they are process consultants and will sit in on meetings, comment on how they are progressing from only a process perspective, but won't say anything about content. At the other end there are consultants who see themselves as content experts in areas such as computer systems. These consultants will look at an organization and tell them exactly what to order, when to order it, and how to order. Again, we

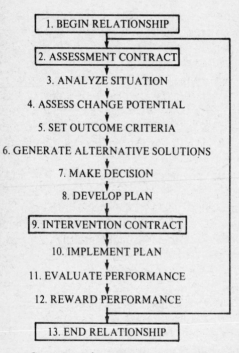

FIGURE 3:3 Consultants' human systems change model

have the same range in the organizational helping area that we have in the individual helping area. Obviously, there is no simple rule. However, I have one question that I find useful. The question is this: "Who has the best information to make a decision?" There is opportunity for us to operate on the whole length of that continuum, depending on the information required. There are some situations in which we need to play more of an expert role because we, in fact, do have the best information. On the other hand there are other situations where specific information is not required and the consultant can play a more facilitative role. The type of response will partially depend on the expectation of the person being helped. For example, if a client wants to be told how many computers to buy and when, and the consultant is simply reflecting on process, the client is going to be very upset. On the other hand, a rebellious teenager is going to be more negatively predisposed to receiving advice. So the situations will vary and it is important for the consultant to maintain flexibility.

Another point to consider in the change process is that the client often develops a temporary dependence on the consultant. Some consultants argue that this should be avoided at all cost, but I believe that it is not necessarily negative, and, at times, can be a very positive factor. A consultant needs to be sensitive to this issue since the dependency can be abused. I have heard consultants say they don't want to be very active because the clients have to learn to do things themselves and shouldn't become dependent. However, I think that sometimes consultants make interventions that are useful and helpful to clients and these interventions do lead to increased dependency. If this occurs it is important to help clients to develop their own skills before terminating the relationship. Sometimes dependency is a necessary stopping point on the road to interdependence and independence.

Another area with regard to change is that there are two critical points at which to intervene. One is at a *systems interface*. The second is at a *time transition*. Let me explain both. By systems interface I mean that problems often occur at the contact point between different parts of a system or between different systems. For instance in a family, problems may occur between the various subsystems (mother-father relationship, father-son relationship). In an organization, problems may occur between various departments (sales and production departments). The reason is that systems have different needs and values; therefore, the interface is often the point of conflict. In terms of time transition, the transition point between events is often a critical and stressful time and, therefore, this is often a time when an intervention is most necessary and can have the most impact. For example, consider attending a meeting. If you look at the time span of the meeting, one of the most critical parts is the first five minutes. How does the meeting begin? Is there an agenda? Is there an agreement to the agenda? Is there a commitment to activities? Another critical transition point in a meeting is the first time a decision is made by the group. How do they make that decision? Is everyone involved in the decision-making process in some way?

However, one caution is appropriate in terms of intervening at time transitions and that relates to developmental transitions. An example would be when a child attends school for the first time. This is a critical and often stressful transition in terms of the child's development, and it is often at such points that there are problems, and some regression. This may be an important time at which to intervene. On the other hand, this is a normal developmental occurance and an intervention would be advised only if the problem were quite serious or prolonged. It is important to note, and this refers to the importance of developmental patterns, that an intervention can have negative as well as positive consequences. Such may be the case for an overreaction to a normal developmental pattern. There are some natural developmental stresses that take care of themselves over time and which don't need as direct and as strong an intervention. The same point applies to organizations. For instance, when one organization merges with another organization you can expect that, over a period of several years, there are going to be some problems. Now that doesn't mean that a consultant shouldn't take any action. But the point is not to think that one situation is so unusual, different or unexpected that you become overly concerned or try to change things too quickly. Some changes take considerable time, and it is necessary to build the intervention cycle into the actual development cycle of that organization.

Another point with regard to change is that different interventions can lead to the same end point. There may be more than one 'correct' intervention. This obviously doesn't mean that any intervention will work equally well in different situations. But there are different possibilities that should be considered and, depending on the situation, some may be more effective in one situation than another.

One final point with regard to the change process is a principle I find useful. I call it 'conservation of power and energy.' It simply means that you personally don't expend more energy or power than you need for any given situation. You expend enough energy and power to accomplish your objectives, but you don't waste either resource. For example, in terms of energy, it is fairly clear that if you can find more efficient ways to accomplish the same results you can expend less energy to accomplish more. That makes sense and gives you more leverage. In terms of power, and this is particularly true for organizational consultants, it is important to have a power base but not to draw upon it unnecessarily. If you are working at a middle level of an organization and you have access to the person on top of the organization who supports you, this gives you added pressure and leverage with regard to the middle level. You don't have to even say anything about it; it never has to come up in conversation, but it can make a big difference. I was working with a division of an organization and the person who was in charge had some mixed feelings about my being there. The people in charge of the total organization wanted me to be there because they were having some problems caused by the division operation being dysfunctional. One of the factors in that situation is that I had access to some additional power, or leverage, but I chose not to use it directly unless absolutely necessary. My sense is that most of the time the fact that the people know about the power base is sufficient.

Having considered some general factors related to the introduction of a consultant to the change process, let us now discuss the four new factors added to the consultants' change model in Figure 3:2: begin relationship; assessment contract; change contract; and, end relationship.

Begin relationship

The first step of the change process is the beginning of the relationship between the consultant and the client. There are several factors that will affect how that relationship gets started. One factor is that the initiation of the contact varies considerably. For example, there is quite a difference between a client who is required to see a consultant as opposed to a client who actually seeks the consulting relationship. At this first stage there is a mutual assessing between the consultant and the client. The client is going to be looking at a couple of factors, although probably not consciously. One is that the client wants to get some idea of whether or not the consultant is competent. This is largely based on the consultant's behavior in the first session. "Was I heard? Did the consultant listen to me? Did the consultant understand what I was saying?" Those are some of the questions. Another factor that is also important is whether the client likes the consultant. "Did I like that person? Did we get along well? Was there a good rapport?" These then are the two main criteria on which clients will tend to assess consultants.

On the other hand, the consultant is also assessing at this initial meeting. This assessing is partially in terms of the potential for change. "Does this individual have some potential for change? What is my initial assessment?" Consultants also go through a similar evaluation in terms of liking. "Is this someone I like? Is this someone I want to work with?" It is also important in this initial session to collect some fundamental information about what the problem is and what is maintaining it, knowing that the assessment may change somewhat at a later point.

One reason why it is important to do this initial assessing before actually attempting to set a contract is to enable the consultant to assess personal skills and experience in order to determine whether or not these qualifications will be sufficient with which to assist a client. One guideline I try to use is to consider various but specific client types (for instance counseling adolescents, consulting with banks, consulting with condominium corporations) and specific problem types (sexual counseling, staff turnover problems, divorce). I then do not accept any clients in which I do not have experience in at least one of the two (client type, problem type) areas. Naturally, I would not work with a problem area that fell outside my training and expertise (for instance, accounting problems in an organization or neuropsychological problems in individual counseling). In these cases I would simply make appropriate referrals.

It is also important at this initial session for the consultant to establish credibility. There is some evidence that the impressions from the initial interview linger, and if the consultant gives an impression of credibility in the first interview there is an improved chance of success. We are initially judged on a number of dimensions including age, sex, and dress. I have been in situations where I was initially perceived as being too young to do whatever it was I was doing. My experience has been that this initial impression loses impact once a task begins and it becomes possible to actually demonstrate competence. However, I do think that it is important that consultants have some idea of what the initial impression likely will be and furthermore have some techniques for dealing with it.

While we can't do very much about our age and sex, we can control our mode of dress. While in the overall scheme of things this is not a terribly important factor, it is an interesting one and it is easily controllable.[5] The key is to wear what is appropriate for the situation. What does your clothing say about you? What would people expect from you on the basis of the way you are dressed? It has been fascinating for me in the past few years to observe dress codes in various organizations. When I was a graduate student I had one pair of jeans and that was it. Now my clients come from a broad range of sectors including international accounting firms, mental health organizations, and correctional centers. Each one has a different dress code. The codes tend not to be in writing (with the exception of correctional centers) but are present nevertheless. For instance, in accounting firms you don't wear a sports jacket because that is too casual; you wear a suit, preferably the navy color and the three piece variety. In correctional centers you don't wear a suit or you would come across as being too formal and proper. The dress of choice would be a navy blue sports jacket with gray slacks, or skirt, because that has a semi-military look. In the mental health institution the dress of choice would be a turtleneck sweater with a sports jacket and slacks or skirt. So you can see that the 'ideal dress' in each of these organizations conveys the image that the organization wants: a proper, respectable accounting firm; a semi-military correctional center; and a casual yet sophisticated mental health institution. My advice would be to recognize the situations and the dress codes and 'when in Rome, dress as the Romans do.' Or at least don't dress in such a way as to discredit yourself. (Ever try to get a contract from an accounting firm while wearing blue jeans?)

Of course the foregoing is not meant to imply that dress establishes credibility. The best way to demonstrate credibility in the first session is in terms of your knowledge and skill in understanding the client and any particular problem. Your awareness of the unique aspects of a particular situation certainly helps. However, actions speak louder than words, and if you can intervene in the first session in some way, your credibility will be further enhanced. It is often important to have one positive, critical incident take place in the first session. Let me give you two examples. I was seeing a family for the first time and they were talking about their problem (mother dominating and father withdrawing) when I noted that this was exactly what was happening in the session. I pointed this out and began to explore some of the factors and behaviors leading up to this incident. Therefore, we were able to actually begin a change process quite early in the session and they felt heard and that the helping process was beginning. Naturally this helped my credibility in this session.

The second incident involved meeting with senior staff of a hospital to discuss a problem they had defined as low staff morale. As we talked it became clear that while there was a slight predictable reduction in staff morale due to budgetary cutbacks, the major problem was the management of the hospital, particularly in terms of communication and decision making. This session allowed them to get further clarification of their situation, and demonstrated to them that I could conceptualize and intervene in such a way as to be helpful to them (credibility is also more than first impressions—the hospital did not hire me to work for them but instead chose a large consulting firm specializing in the health field).

The final point in terms of beginning the relationship is that the session often creates hope for the client. This doesn't necessarily imply that the client was distraught and distressed before the session, but sometimes just feels better having talked with the consultant. This point was so clear to me when I first started in business. I decided I was going to look after my accounting books myself because I thought I should learn how to keep them before I asked someone else to do it. I was setting up the books and I had a confusing array of papers and numbers in front of me, and finally I phoned my accountant and said, "I don't know what to do with this, and I am wondering about this, and I am wondering about that." He talked with me for about fifteen minutes. All that really happened was that I told him what my problems were and on the other end of the line he was saying, "Yes," asking me a few questions. Toward the end of the call he said there were some things he could tell me about right now and others that he wanted to check out. He suggested we get together the following Tuesday and we would clarify all of the issues. I agreed to this suggestion and hung up the phone and felt so much better. He hadn't actually done anything for me yet, but I was really hopeful. I felt that I would be well taken care of. That one incident was so striking in demonstrating the power of a consultant in creating hope.

Assessment contract

The next stage that is different from our previous model is the assessment contract. This contract is clear in organization consulting although it is sometimes less clear in counseling and psychotherapy. The assessment contract is essentially a contract to assess a problem and specifies what type of information will be provided and to whom. At an intrapersonal level this may mean taking a couple of sessions to explore the problem and perhaps complete some psychological tests. At an organizational level it could mean interviewing people, putting some data together and making a recommendation. But it is basically a contract to do assessment as opposed to a change implementation. This distinction can only be made theoretically since whenever one begins assessing, client's expectations change and this may lead to other changes. Often it is more effective to have two contracts rather than one. An example would be a penitentiary for which I was asked to do some organization change work. I said that I would spend a week there and analyze the situation and then write a report for them (assessment contract). I would tell them what I thought they should do on the basis of observation and interviews. It was quite clear that subsequently, if we were both agreeable, we would enter into another contract (change contract) in which I would assist them with the actual change process. But initially we only set up this one contract and then they had a choice point where they could hire someone else to help with the change process or do it themselves.

Intervention contract

The next stage that is different in this model is the change contract. The change contract relates to the implementation and clarifies what is to be accomplished—the objectives, the process time frame, the resources required in time and energy of both the consultant and the client, and the fees.

End relationship

The final step to be mentioned in this chapter is the termination or ending of the relationship with the client. The general objective is that the client will have the skills that are necessary in order to continue or maintain the change that has taken place. I would like a client to develop enough skills to be able to cope with a similar problem in the future. I think the easier goal is to have helped to solve the current problem, but being able to cope is often, in the long run, more important.

It seems appropriate to end with an Amerindian saying which conveys this point very well. Loosely translated it says "If you give me a fish, I eat for a day; if you teach me to fish, I eat for a life-time."

NOTES

1. The term *interaction* refers to the relationship between two systems. It often involves sequences of two events (mother gets angry, father gets angry, etc.).
2. The term *transaction* refers to the relationship between more than two systems. It often involves sequences of three or more events (mother gets angry, child cries, father gets distracted).
3. This concern with the interaction of persons and situations can be found in *Personality at the Crossroads: Current issues in interactional psychology*, D. Magnusson and N.S. Endler, eds. (Hillsdale, N.J.: Lawrence Erlbaum Associates, 1977).
4. The distinction made between *process* and *content* is that content refers to what is being said (I say "Would you close the door, please?") and process refers to how it happens (I feel chilled and speak politely to you).
5. While there is little research in this area an interesting book is *Dress for Success* by John T. Molloy (New York: Warner Books, 1976). He emphasizes a conservative approach relating to current modes of dress.

QUESTIONS

1. A consultant's human systems assessment model is presented in Figure 3:1. Discuss the dimensions of this model. Are there aspects of the model you would add, delete or modify? Explain.
2. Use the model to assess a client-consultant relationship in which you were involved.
3. A consultant's human systems change model is present in Figure 3:3. Use the model to describe a change process in which you were involved. In doing this are there aspects of the model that you would like to modify? Explain.
4. This model adds four new steps to the change model presented in the previous chapter. For each of these steps list the major strategies for success and the major pitfalls to be avoided.
5. It was stated in this chapter that critical intervention points are systems interfaces and time transitions. Analyze a consulting situation in which you were involved in terms of these two dimensions. As a result of this analysis should your intervention be modified?

ANNOTATED BIBLIOGRAPHY

Caplan, G. *The Theory and Practice of Mental Health Consultation*. New York: Basic Books, 1970.
A comprehensive look at consultation from the perspective of the mental health profession.

Lippitt, G. & Lippitt, R. *The Consulting Process in Action*. La Jolla, Ca.: University Associates, 1978.
An easy-to-read yet comprehensive look at the consulting process and the role of the consultant.

PART TWO

We have now completed developing models of how human systems function (Chapter One) and how they change (Chapter Two). We have also modified these models to serve as consultants' models of human systems assessment and human systems change (Chapter Three). It is possible to apply these models to each of the seven human systems levels (intrapersonal, interpersonal, group, intergroup, organization, interorganization, and community). However, there are unique aspects to each of the seven systems levels which require that consultants be aware of the differences as well as the similarities.

In order to gain more awareness of the similarities and differences in applying the models to the seven systems levels, Part Two of this book will devote a chapter to this application for each of the seven systems levels. We begin with the intrapersonal level in Chapter Four and conclude with the community level in Chapter Ten. Each chapter provides both a discussion of the application of the model and examples from the author's practice. In order to avoid redundancy, only Chapter Four will include all steps of the model; subsequent chapters will only consider the assessment (analyze situation [step 2] and assess change potential [step 3]) and the intervention (implement plan [step 10]) aspects.

CHAPTER FOUR

Intrapersonal change

In this chapter we apply the thirteen-step consultants' human systems change model (Figure 3:3) to change at the intrapersonal level.

Begin relationship

The beginning of the relationship between the client and the consultant varies every time in terms of: type of problem, urgency, expectations, rapport, and the time and place of the initial meeting. It is necessary for the consultant to work very hard at understanding the stated problem of the client and take in a tremendous number of clues without jumping to any premature conclusions. The ability to remain in a suspended state of developing some tentative hypotheses about the client without stereotyping or labeling is very important at this stage.

It is important to note, and this supports the fact that the consultant should not jump too quickly, that the presenting problem (the problem the client supposedly has) is often not the real problem. This happens for two main reasons. The first is that often there is a testing period before the client feels comfortable enough discussing a very personal issue. I can recall two examples of this. One situation was a student coming in ostensibly to discuss low grades and, shortly thereafter, relating serious family problems (of which the low grades were but a symptom). Another situation was having two sessions with the client discussing depression before homosexuality was mentioned, which was the major issue of concern. The second reason that often clients do not discuss the real problem initially is that they really do not know what it is. They often have a vague (and sometimes acute) feeling that something is wrong, but they cannot accurately define or label it.

Assessment contract

In the area of individual counseling there is often not a clear distinction between the assessment and the intervention. These two processes are often delicately interwoven during the course of the helping relationship. Therefore, it is not appropriate to make as sharp a distinction between them in these individual situations as it would be at the organizational level.

On the other hand, many individual counselors fail to set contracts with clients at times when it is appropriate to do so. They do not set specific contracts related to assessment, do not set explicit change contracts based on assessments, and do not make explicit changes in the contract as the sessions continue and the understanding of the problems and their interrelationships become clearer. They drift along, dealing with whatever comes up, with no sense of direction or purpose. I believe that it is often necessary to set contracts related to an initial assessment, and to subsequently set up contracts around the implementation as required.

Analyze situation

The consultant's human systems assessment model for the intrapersonal level is shown in Figure 4:1. This model is appropriate to apply to general human systems functioning. However, before moving into the specifics of the model, it is important to note that consultants will need other models and techniques of assessment as well. For instance, if specific questions arise relative to psychological functioning, it may be useful to incorporate psychological testing. If there is a question relative to neurological functioning, it is important to include a neurological assessment. If there are financial problems, it is important to do an assessment of income and expenditures. Naturally, the initial consultant would not be expected to perform all these functions. However, the consultant should be aware of some of the signs of potential problems in various areas and be able to call in appropriate professional expertise as required.

Therefore, in terms of the more general aspects of the intrapersonal level, let us consider the model:

1) Systems level: intrapersonal

2) Systems analysis:
   a) Input
   b) Throughput
   c) Output
   d) Feedback
   e) Boundary
   f) Environment

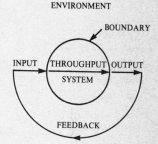

3) Developmental stage

4) General factors:
   a) Objectives
   b) Structure
   c) Roles
   d) Communication
   e) Reward system
   f) Power
   g) Time
   h) Space

5) Client-consultant relationship

FIGURE 4:1 Consultants' human systems assessment model: intrapersonal level

Systems level

The systems level we are considering is intrapersonal.

Systems analysis

There are six aspects to systems analysis: input; throughput; output; feedback; boundary; and, environment.

Input

In terms of input the question to ask would be, "What is this individual taking in?" Are there deficits or dysfunctional surpluses? For instance, one important input is food. Unfortunately, unless one happens to be a dietician or a nutritionist, this aspect is seldom considered. However, it is important and can have tremendous psychological and physiological effects. Another important input is information. Is there sufficient intellectual stimulation? In terms of affect, does this individual receive sufficient (in quantitative and qualitative terms) emotional stimulation? Another question is whether the individual receives sufficient physical stimulation. Babies can actually die through lack of stimulation. A related question is whether or not an individual has sufficient exercise. This can significantly affect an individual's functioning. It is also important to note that an individual is also an economic being. Therefore, another question is whether there is sufficient financial input. Put more simply, is enough money being made? Many personal problems are related to lack of money. If people don't have enough money to house themselves, to feed themselves, to clothe themselves and provide some amenities of life, they will likely suffer some form of stress.

Throughput

Throughput also presents several processes to consider. One is how individuals think—their cognitive process. Another is how they feel—their affective process. Another, related to these and also related to input to some extent, is their perceptual process. How do they see the world? We all know people who see things very positively and other people who see things very negatively. So it is not just what the 'real' input is; it is also how this input is perceived. And of course, there are the many aspects of physiological process.

These may have significant effects on behavior. Extreme examples are people who have brain lesions, or brain tumors, or serious nervous system disorders. However, even more minor factors such as headaches can affect behavior.

One important aspect of individual functioning that can be related to throughput is the individuals' defenses.[1] What defense mechanisms does an individual employ for protection? It should be noted that we all utilize defense mechanisms, and these are important to our functioning. The object is not to destroy defense mechanisms (as encounter groups have been accused, with some justification, of doing) but rather to assist individuals to utilize defense mechanisms which involve the least possible distortion in an individual's level of functioning.

Output

In terms of output, one of the main factors to consider is work. Does an individual work? make a 'contribution' to society? Another aspect of output might be the support that an individual gives to other people. An economist would say financial output of an individual is important. An environmentalist might say that an important output of an individual is pollution. A physiologist would say an important output is carbon dioxide. There are many outputs that an individual creates, and one of the questions at this point becomes "How appropriate are these outputs for the environment that the individual is in?" do they fit? is there some kind of connection? The answer is always changing. Take cigarette smoking as an example. A few years ago anyone could smoke anywhere. Now there are many places where smoking is prohibited. In terms of pollution what's acceptable and what isn't in terms of the environment has shifted over the past few years. An individual's smoking in a theatre a few years ago was considered acceptable behavior. Today it is not. The smoker could be fined. So it is important to change behaviors in light of changing environmental demands. Another example is in terms of work output. This must be assessed in terms of society's norms and values. For instance, some people have certain middle class values that require people to work; others do not. I have done some work with native peoples in Canada, many of whom have very different value systems. They're not better or worse, but different. There are some things about their value system that I like, which I wish we encouraged more, such as cooperativeness and support. There are some things that I, personally, don't like. But, here I am assessing on the basis of my value system and it is important to assess output on the basis of the actual environmental demands. If these demands are considered inappropriate, alternate strategies such as removing an individual from an environment or changing the environment could be considered.

Feedback

Another important aspect in assessing an individual is the nature of the feedback the individual receives. We all have physiological feedback systems. We have a middle ear which helps to give us balance. When our body temperature gets too high, we perspire. We also have other types of feedback systems. Friends and family may give us feedback on what they like and don't like about us. We get a performance appraisal at work. Our bank manager gives us a loan. A driver honks at us when we cut him off on the road. These are all examples of types of feedback we receive.

Boundary

In terms of the boundary between an individual and the environment, the critical question relates to how open or closed the boundary is. An individual with a very rigid boundary may be quite compulsive and not make very good contact with the environment. This person would be isolated and, in the extreme, may live the life of a hermit. At the other extreme you find a very loose boundary. In this case the individual would be other-oriented, disorganized, overly dependent and perhaps bordering on hysterical behavior. It would, therefore, be important to determine any gross deficiencies in this area which may contribute to problems.

Environment

There are certain important aspects of an environment for any given individual. These may include people with whom the individual has relationships, or certain situations such as work. They may involve certain family members including both the immediate and extended families. It is important to determine significant factors in the environment, and to understand the demands that different parts of the environment make. This is especially important where there are conflicting demands from the individual's environment. For instance, a classic situation in our society is an individual who has demands to spend long hours on the job and a lot of time with the family.

Developmental stage

The third aspect of the model involves consideration of the developmental stage. This is an important factor in any attempt to assess an individual and the literature here is better than at any other human systems level. While there has been for a long time considerable literature on the developmental stages of children and adolescents, more recently there has been more useful material on adult life stages.[2] While it is certainly beyond the scope of this book to present or discuss this material, the consultant should be aware that it can be very helpful in determining the appropriateness of behavior in certain situations.

General factors

Eight general factors are considered in the model. These include: objectives; structure; roles; communication; reward system; power; time; and, space. Each of these factors will not be discussed at the intrapersonal level.

Objectives

In terms of time perspective it is important for people to have a future time orientation; something in the future to look forward to, some meaning, some striving. Therefore, it is important to determine whether an individual has objectives. There is considerable literature showing that one of the factors related to apathy and alienation is the lack of meaningful objectives. Does the individual have something to strive for? Is there something that gives life meaning? It doesn't have to be a great thing like becoming a doctor or an astronaut. Many simple things give us meaning, such as taking a special interest course, or developing a hobby or even meeting a friend. So, minor areas can be involved as well as major ones, but it is important that people are in a 'process of becoming' rather than just being stagnant.

It is interesting to note that in our society there is a custom that supports this idea, except it is a very misused custom. That is the

New Year's resolution. Making New Year's resolutions is a great idea. Sit down at least once a year and ask "What am I doing? What do I want? How can I do it?" Unfortunately, rather than setting realistic objectives we set unrealistic ones such as stopping smoking soon or losing 20 pounds next week.

Structure

Structure is used in this book to refer to the representation of relationships between people such as is found on an organization chart. Therefore, this term is not relevant at the intrapersonal level.

Roles

From the initial analysis of the person as a system, the relationship to the environment, and the important people in the environment, it should be possible to develop further information about roles. It is particularly important to determine whether roles are clear and whether there is a conflict or an incompatability among the different roles that an individual must play. In our society we play many roles including those of mothers, fathers, daughters, sons, professionals, friends, and clients. If we ever stopped and added up the number of different roles we play in different situations, we would probably be surprised; we would find the number high and each role carries certain expectations. For instance, we play the customer role in a restaurant, and know that certain forms of behavior in that situation are acceptable and others are not. For instance, the movie "Bob & Carol, Ted & Alice" humorously pointed out that it is not acceptable behavior for customers to go into the kitchen and talk to the chef in a highly personal manner.

Communication

We have said that communication might be cognitive or affective or physical. One of the main functions of the consultant is to assess the communication of the human system. Communication is a two-way process so we must assess it in terms of both receiving and sending information. In terms of receiving information, the questions are "Does the client really hear me? Does the client really take in what I am saying? Do I get through to this person? Is there some contact?" In terms of sending information the question would be whether or not the messages the client is sending are clear, concise and understandable. Is the message congruent? Or are you receiving mixed messages?

It is also important to assess the balance of cognitive, affective and physical, or non-verbal, communication. Many clients in counseling sessions experience problems of an affective or emotional or feeling nature: "I get mad at people." or, "I can't express warm feelings to people." or, "I get embarrassed if someone says something nice to me." or, "I am afraid to stand up and be assertive." or, "I get anxious and I can't do that." But while the affective areas are very important, they are difficult for most people to discuss and therefore are often avoided.

Another responsibility of the consultant is to look for any incongruence. An example would be someone saying, "I really like that person," with their teeth clenched and their hand in a fist. The verbal and physical messages are incongruent. Another example would be, when someone is feeling sad but they say that they feel fine, you sometimes hear the voice breaking. If I had to choose one medium to believe, I would choose the non-verbal over the verbal 99 per cent of the time. It is harder to dissemble physically than to lie with the words.

It is also important to attend to the non-verbal communication. This area is very faddish right now with many absolute answers being given. If you sit or stand a certain way you are an uptight person and if you stand or sit another way you are pretty loose and okay. It is quite possible to read too much into this area and attribute things to individuals that are not there. However, there are some clues which, if taken in the context of the situation, can be useful. For instance, if someone shifts body position at a stressful moment this may be supportive evidence that they are feeling the stress.

Reward system

At an individual level this involves looking at both levels of motivation (what are the needs, wants and desires) and the reward system (what is rewarded and punished?) in the environment. Both are important and often the environmental analysis is ignored. For instance, in working with an offender who comes from a family and community where there are no strong norms against breaking the law, a consultant, in order to assist the individual in changing these patterns has to develop strategies for countering the norm. The failure to do this is one of the reasons that many well-intentioned attempts to help eventually fail.

Power

The basic question relates to whether the individual has the personal power necessary to meet objectives. In situations where this is not the case, one change strategy is assertiveness training.[3] Assertiveness training is a special technique that deals with this particular area of power, that helps an individual to be more assertive and demonstrate more personal power. The training usually involves role-playing in which participants practice handling difficult situations. Another aspect of personal power relates to a person's locus of control.[4] *Locus of control* ranges on a scale from internal to external. People with internal locus of control believe they have considerable control over life, and can significantly structure their environment. People with external locus of control, on the other hand, believe that although they do their best the environment often isn't very supportive and anyway, we are so controlled by the government and the organizations we work for that there is probably not very much point in trying to do very much. In such a situation a consultant needs to help a client develop enough of an internal locus of control to be able to effect the sort of change that would be desirable.

Time

This factor involves past, present and future time frames. In terms of the past, a consultant should have information about important client history; in terms of the present, a consultant should collect information based on observations and client's self-reports; in terms of the future, a consultant should assist in developing objectives and plans to meet these objectives. All three time frames are important and should be considered.

Space

At the intrapersonal level we should focus on the individual's physical environment. How does the environment look, sound and smell? What does it do to enhance or detract from the objectives? Is the individual's environment functional? Can it be modified? If not, can the client develop a new space (move to another house or another neighborhood)?

Client-consultant relationship

A consultant has to assess the relationship on an ongoing basis. The relationship in many cases is critical in terms of assessing and maintaining the change process. Difficulties or problems in the relationship should be discussed since they can be blocks that will hamper progress.

Let us look at the client-consultant relationship in terms of three factors: feedback, time, and space. Feedback is a critical part of the client-consultant relationship. You should be able to give good feedback yet, this is rare. By good feedback I mean feedback that is specific, accurate, and to the point. We tend not to get very good feedback from people about how we are doing. That is one of the reasons why close relationships are so important, because in close relationships hopefully you can get the kind of feedback you don't get otherwise. You don't get good feedback from acquaintances. You probably don't get it from friends; you probably don't get it at work. This is unfortunate since the effectiveness of an individual's functioning is very related to the quality of feedback received. One of the things a consultant can do is to work on the quality of feedback. How can you get better feedback? How can you build a better feedback system for yourself? How can you get people to be more honest with you in terms of the feedback you do receive? This is critical for individuals, and is often inadequate.

Both time and space become important when a consultant schedules meetings. The tendency is to schedule regular appointments (often once a week) in the consultant's office. This approach naturally is most advantageous to the consultant who can schedule time effectively and does not have to worry about travel. However, I would advocate consideration of two modifications to this practice. The first is that it is often useful to hold an early session in the home of the client. This gives the consultant a much better picture of the client's environment and offers the potential for a more comprehensive assessment. I would also suggest that some flexibility be given to the scheduling of appointments. Dealing with critical events in a closer time proximity can be more advantageous than always waiting exactly seven days. However, it is obvious that caution would have to be exercised in adopting either of these suggestions. There are some situations where there would be little advantage in assessing the individual's environment, and there are some situations where clients would use the scheduling of appointments as a manipulation.

64

Assess change potential

Change potential needs to be assessed in terms of motivation, skills, and power. In terms of motivation, it is often appropriate to consider how much 'pain' an individual is in. There is considerable data to indicate that individuals in crisis situations are more likely to change than individuals in more normal situations. Another factor related to motivation is the history of the problem. Generally speaking, a problem of a more recent nature, even when it is quite serious (acute), has a greater probability of being solved than one of longer duration (chronic). I have seen individuals who have been in and out of therapy for over ten years with a problem, and some of the side-effects. Obviously, the client's chances in such situations are not very good.

In terms of skills, we have a good opportunity to assess an individual during our meeting. We can consider any skill areas that seem to be related to the problem. These could include communication, problem solving and decision making. It is also useful to assess whether an individual has the potential to learn any required skills.

In terms of power, we are usually concerned with personal power issues. Does the individual have sufficient ego strength and confidence to make the necessary changes? How much support will be necessary?

Set outcome criteria

Generate alternative solutions

Make decision

Develop plan

These four categories are considered simultaneously since at the intrapersonal level they often merge in the ongoing interaction between the client and the consultant. It is useful to ask basic questions such as "What do you want? What are different ways of getting it? What are you going to do? and, What steps do you need to go through?"

It should be noted that the consultant will usually not recommend specific changes to a client. Often the consultant will assist clients to come to their own answers. There are several reasons for this. In the first place, the client will have to live with the decision, so in most cases the client is the best person to make the decision. In the second place, part of the problem is often that the client is unable to reach a decision, and the experience of making the decision can be beneficial in itself. Finally, if the client makes the decision there tends to be more commitment to its implementation.

The consultant can often play an important role during this stage in acting as a reality check for the client. Sometimes the criteria, solutions, decision or plan may not be very realistic, and the consultant can assist the client to develop awareness of potential pitfalls. Of course, sometimes the client needs to experience the plan and learn from any mistakes, so the consultant does not always (and cannot always) play this forewarning role.

Intervention contract

This is the contract pertaining to the actual counseling or consulting process. It will usually include factors such as dates; times and places of sessions; fees involved; services provided; areas to be covered in the sessions; and, specific objectives to be accomplished. At times this contract will be distinct from the assessment contract and at times both contracts will merge.

It must be re-emphasized that the distinction between the two contracts is not absolute. Just as the assessment contract has some intervention impact, there is an ongoing assessment built into the intervention process. The situation is constantly changing and the consultant must be alert to new facts which may require modifications in the change process.

Implement plan

The implementation process centers on the interaction between the consultant and the client. Several points need to be made about this interaction. The first is that there must be an information exchange between the two, and the clarity of messages sent and received by both will be critical to the success of the process. The second is that a relationship must be established between the two, and the affective aspects of this relationship (liking and respecting the other) will be important to the outcome. The third point is that there is a mutually influencing system; it is not only the client who will be influenced by the consultant (although this is the part most discussed in counseling research literature) but also the consultant by the client.

In considering the level of communication taking place we can conclude that there are two levels operating: intrapersonal and interpersonal. Intrapersonal communication is taking place within both the consultant and the client. (What am I feeling?) Many counseling and therapy processes emphasize the intrapersonal aspects (the Gestalt hot seat; psychoanalytic free association) for the client. It is obvious this level is also important for the consultant, for a lack of self-awareness can be a major impediment to assisting another person.

There is also a level of interpersonal communication. Information is transmitted back and forth between the two. In this interaction certain consultant behaviors are generally thought to be desirable. These include trying to really understand the other person's position (this is harder than it sounds); respecting the other person; being honest (while at the same time being supportive); disclosing oneself (so the relationship isn't totally one-sided); confronting (as required); dealing with here-and-now material; and interpretation and advice (in moderate degrees).

However, it is often necessary to go beyond the verbal interaction in order for the change process to be successful. It is important for the client to, as much as possible, experience a situation as opposed to only talking about it. For instance, instead of talking about what it would feel like to stand up to the boss, actually doing it in a role-playing situation. This change strategy could be preceded by having someone demonstrate helpful behaviors. This is a useful strategy since much of our learning comes from imitating models (for instance a young child imitating the behavior of one of the parents).

Probably the most important and most overlooked aspect of the change process is the transfer of the new and improved behavior to the outside situation. Often this is ignored since it is assumed that a behavior that can be performed in one situation can be performed in another. However, this is often not the case, and it is important to work on the transfer. One way of doing this is to give the client homework assignments pertaining to the behavior (for instance, role-playing talking to a friend in the session and actually talking to the friend in real life and reporting back).

One final note. There is a tendency for these sessions to focus only on the negative and provide little reinforcement and support for the positive. A serious imbalance of this nature can create many problems.

Evaluate performance

While most consultants will not have the resources or perhaps even the inclination to do sophisticated research, some basic evaluative procedures are recommended. One of the best ways of evaluating is to determine whether your clients are meeting their objectives (and if they don't have any, you are not meeting yours). Another is to do telephone follow-ups 6-12 months after the completion of the sessions. But one of the most valuable follow-ups is also the most difficult. It is to follow-up with those who terminated before completion. They may provide the best information about areas that we, as consultants, could improve upon.

Reward performance

Once the evaluation has determined that there is a change it is important to make sure that the reward system will maintain the change. This does not, of course, imply that this issue should only be considered now. On the contrary, now is simply a time to determine if the reward system is behaving in the anticipated manner, and if not, to make appropriate modifications. The basic question to ask is whether the individual is receiving sufficient internal (personal satisfaction) and external (support, confirmation) reward to maintain the change.

End relationship

The ending of a counseling relationship often raises some anxiety due to the loss of dependence and support. It is important to determine that the client not only has sufficient skills but also the self-confidence to continue and maintain the process.

68

NOTES

1. While Sigmund Freud originated the concept of defenses, his daughter, Anna Freud, set out one of the clearest early descriptions in *The Ego and the Mechanisms of Defense* rev. ed. (*The Writings of Anna Freud*, Vol. 2). (New York: International Universities Press, 1967).
2. While several books are worthy of consideration, Gail Shelley's *Passages* (New York: Bantam Books, 1977) is a very readable yet quite thorough look at the stages and crises of adult life.
3. A further discussion of assertiveness training can be found in *Your Perfect Right: A guide to assertive behavior*, by R.E. Alberti and M.L. Emmons (San Luis Obispo: Impact, 1974).
4. A comprehensive treatment of this area can be found in *Locus of Control in Personality* by E.J. Phares (Morristown, N.J.: General Learning Press, 1976)

QUESTIONS

1. Are you explicit in contracting with your clients? Do you use both the assessment contract and the change contract? Describe your approach.
2. Apply the assessment model to yourself. What do you learn about strengths and weaknesses of the model? What do you learn about yourself?
3. Consider situations in which the counseling process has not succeeded. Using the model of assessing change potential, determine whether the reasons were lack of skill, motivation or power. What initial strategies could be used to cut down the failure rate?
4. Develop your own model of intrapersonal change.
5. How thoroughly do you evaluate your change work? What improvements could be made?

70

ANNOTATED BIBLIOGRAPHY

Annual Review of Psychology

One of the best values around. Describes the state of the art in individual change and other related areas.

Bandler, R. & Grinder, J. *The Structure of Magic*. 2 vols. Palo Alto: Science and Behavior Books, 1976.

Through the structure of language these authors develop an innovative system to assist in understanding the communication process and the change process.

Carkhuff, R.R. *Helping and Human Relations*. 2 vols. New York: Holt, Rinehart & Winston, 1969.

Describes an excellent system for training and developing communication skills, based on the work of Carl Rogers.

Clark, T. & Jaffe, D.T. *Toward a Radical Therapy*. New York: Gordon & Breach, 1973.

The authors of this book discuss many of the links between individual and social change and describe the need for, and their attempts to provide, alternative services for both personal and social change.

Lazarus, A.A. *Multimodal Behavior Therapy*. New York: Springer, 1976.

A significant step in integrating various treatment modalities. Lazarus outlines and describes treating the BASIC ID (Behavior, Affect, Sensation, Imagery, Cognition, Interpersonal Relationships and Drugs).

Polster, E. & Polster, M. *Gestalt Therapy Integrated*. New York: Brunner/Mazel, 1973.

An excellent description of the Gestalt Therapy process.

Turner, Francis J. *Psychosocial Therapy: A social work perspective*. New York: Free Press, 1978.

An excellent book describing a multi-model approach to treatment taking into account both intrapsychic and environmental factors.

CHAPTER FIVE

Interpersonal change

There is relatively little literature on interpersonal change. The assumption is often made that the focus of change is on the individual, and working with two individuals simply involves having two individual sessions in tandem. This assumption is often not correct, and the process of assessment and intervention differs at the interpersonal level from that at the intrapersonal level.

The best developed body of literature at the interpersonal level comes from the marriage counseling and therapy fields. However, many of the insights from this area also apply to interpersonal situations stemming from group, organization or community interaction. Therefore, in discussing the interpersonal system we will initially consider the marital relationship and later look at the implication for other types of change situations, in particular a boss-subordinate relationship in an organization. We will first consider the assessment perspective, and later look at the intervention implications.

Assessment

The human systems assessment model for the interpersonal level is presented in Figure 5:1. The model is the same as for the intrapersonal level and involves a systems analysis (input, throughput, output, feedback, boundary, and environment); consideration of the developmental stage; consideration of eight general factors (objectives, structure, roles, communication, reward system, power, time, and space); and the client-consultant relationship.

Understanding the functioning of the interpersonal system is more complex than understanding the functioning of the intrapersonal system. This is because it is necessary to consider both the intrapersonal aspects as well as the interpersonal aspects. The inter-

1) Systems level: interpersonal

2) Systems analysis:
   a) Input
   b) Throughput
   c) Output
   d) Feedback
   e) Boundary
   f) Environment

3) Developmental stage

4) General factors:
   a) Objectives
   b) Structure
   c) Roles
   d) Communication
   e) Reward System
   f) Power
   g) Time
   h) Space

5) Client-consultant relationship

FIGURE 5:1 Consultants' human systems assessment model: interpersonal level

personal system is shown in Figure 5:2. As can be seen, we start with two intrapersonal systems, both of which have input, through-put, output, feedback, boundary, and an environment. When these two systems become linked (the output of one becomes the input of the other and vice versa), we can conceptualize the two of them as forming a new system. This system itself then has input, through-put, output, feedback, a boundary, and an environment. It is, there-fore, necessary to be able to assess them both at the intrapersonal level (considered in Chapter 4) and at the interpersonal level (considered in this chapter). The interpersonal system takes on an identity which is related but not identical to the sum of the two individuals in it.

Marital interpersonal system[1]

We will first consider a marital interpersonal system and later con-sider a boss-subordinate interpersonal system.

Systems level

The human systems level being considered is interpersonal.

Systems analysis

As indicated in Figure 5:2, the interpersonal system has input, throughput, output, feedback, a boundary, and an environment.

In terms of input into the interpersonal system we must consider cognitive, affective and physical stimulation as well as financial in-put (the money the couple earns). It is important that there be sufficient input so that the system does not over-rely on itself for stimulation. In today's highly mobile society in which individuals are cut off from their roots there is often a tendency to expect too much from the relationship; this often results in stress on the sys-tem and disappointment in the outcome.

Another type of input that is important is the expectation the two people have about the relationship. This is determined both by pre-vious experience (comparing it with the relationship of the parents) and current values and pressures (societal norms around degree of honesty and intimacy, degree of sexual fulfillment).

In terms of throughput we must consider the interaction between the two individuals. Their communication and problem-solving and

74

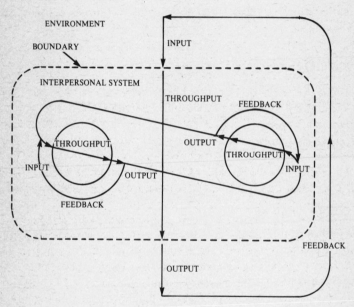

FIGURE 5:2 Interpersonal human system

decision-making patterns are significant parts of the throughput.

In terms of output we can consider factors ranging from work to financial expenditures to having children $(1 + 1 = 3)$.

In terms of feedback, the couple receives feedback from various sources. Certainly the feedback from immediate family including siblings and especially from parents remains important. The couple will also receive feedback from friends. As well, the couple in a less direct way receives feedback from society generally. For instance, television and advertising provide feedback as to how the couple is doing compared with various implied standards and values.

As indicated in Figure 5:2, the couple has a boundary around itself, separating itself from the environment. One of the issues for any couple is how rigid to make the boundary. For instance, a couple who does everything themselves and does not have much contact with the environment would be considered to have a relatively rigid boundary. This may be referred to as 'folie a deux' where the two partners become so enamored with each other that they lose perspective. On the other hand, a couple could have few rules or requirements for each other and not spend very much time together. This would create a very loose boundary, and one would have to question whether an intimate relationship actually existed. Clearly couples choose (usually without being aware of the choice) the rigidness or looseness of this boundary.

The final systems aspect is the environment. An interesting fact about the environment for an interpersonal human system is that part of the environment is similar for the two people and part of it is different. For instance each person would have in common certain friends and family. However, each would have exclusive contact with parts of the environment which might include the people each knew at their places of work and certain members of their family of origin.

Developmental stage

The third part of the model involves considering the developmental stage of the couple. Unfortunately, there is no single comprehensive system for doing so. The stages that couples go through are to some extent defined by individual and family stages. This includes how long the couple has been together; whether the relationship is at a courting stage or honeymoon stage or the seven-year questioning stage and decisions relating to having and not having children.

Different crises tend to be faced at different stages and, therefore, this information is important. However, reference must usually be made to the intrapersonal and family stages.

General Factors

In terms of the third part of this model, several areas should be considered. The first one would be the objectives of the relationship. What does the couple want to attain? What type of lifestyle do they desire? This is obviously difficult because they are two individuals with two different sets of values and needs, coming together and arriving at some kind of mutuality. How do they arrive at that point? What kinds of compromises and trade-offs do they make? What objectives do they have in common that are important? In order for a couple to stay together they have to have enough objectives in common. If the unique personal objectives are too different from the common objectives of the couple, the negative pressure on the relationship may be too much.

The second aspect we will consider is structure. Structure is really quite simple. There are two people in a relationship and a boundary around them. The structural aspects of a human system do not take on much significance until we get to more complex levels of human systems.

In terms of roles, we have an area that often indicates problems. Ten years ago it was fairly clear what roles people should take in our society. However, there have been considerable changes over this period of time. There are many more options. The issue of what roles these two people are going to play relative to each other becomes a very important issue. "Who is going to work? Will there be any children? Who is going to look after the children?" These are some of the basic issues to be resolved. There has to be development and clarification of the roles and a mutual adherence to the decisions.

One of the keys to resolution in the area of roles as well as in other areas is communication. In terms of communication there should be a balance between the cognitive, affective and physical. In terms of the cognitive, there is a need for a certain amount of information sharing, decision making and intellectual stimulation. In terms of the affective or emotional relationship, one of the purposes of a marriage or a close relationship between two people is to provide emotional or affective contact. This is usually either an implicit or explicit objective of the relationship. The third aspect of communication, physical, is important in two main ways. One is simply in terms of affection: touching, holding, and caressing. The other is the sexual relationship, which is an important part of a marital relationship and can also be either a symptom or a cause of marital problems.

The next area to consider is the reward system or motivation in a marital relationship. "What are the rewards in the relationship? What is the motivation of the partners? What is the satisfaction? How do the partners reward and punish each other?" At a very simple level, presumably the satisfaction, or rewards, have to outweigh the dissatisfaction, or the negative aspects.

Another potential area of problems is the power distribution between these two people. Traditionally, the male tended to have the power role. Now power tends to be more divided and mutual in marital relationships. It becomes necessary to determine the power base for each spouse. "What resources does each partner control that gives her/him power? What is the power balance in the relationship? How do the spouses feel about it?"

The next dimension to consider is time. There are several ways that this dimension is important in interpersonal relations. One of the most common problems is dissension in how a couple spends time. Time is a precious resource and, like other resources, how it is spent is very important. Another important aspect of time in a relationship is the time orientation of the partners. Whether they tend to be more present, past or future oriented. For instance, if one tends to be more present oriented the concerns are with the satisfactions of today, with living life fully today. If one has more of a future orientation the concerns are with planning for the future, making sure that things will be better three or five years down the road. Often there is a conflict between those two orientations. One of the partners will say "You're always working, why don't you just relax and enjoy yourself?" and the other partner will say, "Well, if I spent as much time doing that as you want, we wouldn't be living here because we wouldn't be able to afford these things." Therefore, strong differences in time orientation can lead to problems.

The next area to consider is space. Among the issues in interpersonal relations is how space is divided and how it is utilized. Is the division fair and does it meet the needs of both individuals? A further question is whether the space usage allows the individuals to have both space to be together and space to be separate. Many problems stem from a lack of separate space.

Client-consultant relationship

The fifth step of the human systems assessment model for the interpersonal level is the client-consultant relationship. This is shown in Figure 5:3. The figure shows a consultant and two clients. It should be noted that each person of this triad has a relationship with each of the other two people. So, instead of having to deal with only one immediate relationship (client/consultant) as in the intrapersonal level, the consultant working at the interpersonal level has to be concerned with three relationships (client A/client B; client A/consultant; and client B/consultant). As well, there is an intrapersonal process within each person. So one can see that the dynamics of this situation become more complex and that the consultant needs to be aware of much more data. This is quite important in understanding the intervention process and will be discussed shortly.

The final factor to consider is the change potential. In assessing the change potential in a marital situation we must consider motivation, skill, and power, the three variables presented in Figure 2:2.

In terms of motivation, a key question would be how much investment the couple seems to have in the relationship. Do they seem to need the relationship and feel that something significant is missing or has been lost, or do they seem more complacent? Are they prepared to take some risks in terms of exploring material that may give rise to pain or uncertainty?

In terms of skill, the key variable to be concerned with is communication. Is it clear and direct? Can the couple express their needs? Can they really hear each other? Can they engage in a mutual problem-solving process?

In terms of power, the key variable would be the distribution of power between the couple. If there is an imbalance of power, does the more powerful partner support the therapy process? If not, the chances for failure and/or sabotage are increased.

Boss-subordinate Interpersonal System

This model can also be used to analyze interpersonal systems other than the marital one just considered. It can be used to consider any relationship between two people. These could include a boss-subordinate relationship in an organization, the relationship between two siblings, the

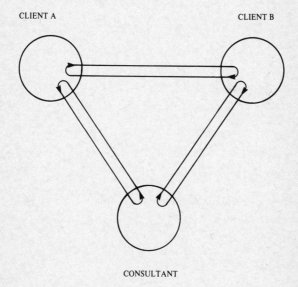

CONSULTANT

FIGURE 5:3 Consultant relationship with interpersonal system

relationship between two siblings, the relationship between two peers or a teacher-student relationship.

Naturally, in these various situations the consultant would come to different conclusions through the systems assessments (Figure 5:1). In order to understand these differences between types of interpersonal systems the second type we will consider is a boss-subordinate relationship. This relationship is selected not only for its different context (organization) but also for its significant differences in other factors (power distribution).

Systems level

The systems level is also interpersonal for a boss-subordinate relationship.

Systems analysis

The systems analysis involves the same six factors (input, throughput, output, feedback, a boundary, and an environment). The input of the relationship would be primarily organization-controled such as directives, organizational norms, and rules and regulations. There would be a great deal of information input. The throughput would tend to be the types of discussions and negotiations between the two individuals. The output would be measured primarily in terms of productivity. There would be feedback of both an informal (discussions with peer groups) and formal (annual performance appraisals) nature. The boundary around the two would be less solid than would typically be the case in a marital situation. The environment would be primarily in terms of the organization: other members of the work team, other departments, and relevant parts of the organization's environment (clients and suppliers).

Developmental stage

The developmental stage in this type of relationship is very difficult to assess. Because these relationships tend to be less personal they do not go through the same stages as a marital relationship. Perhaps one of the major considerations is the length of time the two have known each other. The beginning stages of an organizational relationship range from suspicion and mistrust to a 'honeymoon effect' in which flaws have not yet surfaced and individuals are overrated.

General factors

There are eight factors to consider: objectives, structure, roles, communication, reward system, power, time, and space.

The basic objective of the relationship is usually to be sufficiently mutually rewarding so as to provide each party with satisfaction. The specifics of the objectives would be determined by organizational objectives and norms.

The structure of the system is simply two people in a relationship and is not a critical factor (as it was not for the marital relationship).

The roles are different from those of the marital relationship in two ways. They are obviously different in content. The role expectations for husband and wife are quite different from those for boss and subordinate. However, they are also different in their degree of explicitness. The boss-subordinate roles are often written out and are discussed and explained in advance of the relationship. Theoretically, one should be able to understand the boss-subordinate role more clearly. Unfortunately, this process is often poorly managed in an organization and the difference is, therefore, not as great as one might expect.

The communication is also different in the boss-subordinate relationship. The main difference is that it tends to be highly channeled along the cognitive lines, and there is generally little overt physical or emotional communication. I say overt because often these areas come through and are picked up at a subconscious level through body language and behaviors indicating how one feels about someone else.

The reward system is also more explicit than it is in a marital relationship. In both types of relationships there is an interdependence and the partners reinforce each other. The boss-subordinate contract is essentially that the boss is to provide support and direction, and the subordinate is to perform assigned tasks competently. Both will, therefore, receive formal (pay, benefits) and informal (sense of accomplishment, friendship) rewards.

Perhaps the most important variable to consider is power. The reality is that while power is seldom absolutely equal, even in a marital relationship, it is much less so in a boss-subordinate relationship. This is a critical point in considering interventions. Consultants usually have a strong belief in the basic equality of all people, and therefore, tend to believe that all people should act, and be treated, as equals. However, it is difficult to act as equals when that, in fact, is not the case; it is difficult to confront the boss when your job is on the line, and this possible organizational reality must be considered in later interventions.

In terms of time, the relationship generally occurs during office hours. One of the issues for managers is whether or not the relationship should go beyond this time to include social contact. There is no correct answer to this problem and depends on the specific situation.

The final factor is space. A boss and subordinate may or may not share common space. If they do you can usually tell who is the boss by the size of the office and the materials in it. If they don't share the same space (superintendent of schools and school principals) the subordinate generally has fewer restrictions, by virtue of this geographic separation.

Client-consultant relationship

The consultant relationship as shown in Figure 5:3 is the same for the boss-subordinate relationship as for the marital relationship in that it involves three intrapersonal systems and three relationships (client A/client B; client A/consultant; client B/consultant).

The final factor to consider is the change potential. In assessing the change potential in a boss-subordinate relationship the same three variables are considered: motivation, skill, and power.

In terms of motivation, the key is to determine the perceived benefits to the participants, compared with the perceived risks. This is an important formula to consider since the decision in this situation is often made on a variation of this formula.

In terms of skill, communication and negotiation skills are critical. Fortunately the skills are, to a large extent, trainable.

In terms of power, the key is whether the person or people in power (the boss or the boss' boss) support the program.

Intervention

Let us move into the actual change process. This is different from the intrapersonal change process. In this process there are two clients (A and B) and a consultant. This process applies to marital situations as well as to other situations such as a boss-subordinate relationship. The marital situation will be considered first.

Marital interpersonal system

The pair have come to you with a problem. If the problem really is primarily of an interpersonal nature it is important that both are involved in the solution since both probably caused, or at least help to maintain, the problem. Inevitably, though, when you run into an interpersonal problem the two parties will nearly always define the problem in terms of the other person. Very seldom does it not happen that way. The husband says, "If only my wife would stop nagging me. That is the root of all the problems." The wife says, "If only my husband would get more involved with me and the kids like he used to be." What you have is an interactive pattern. It is not one person causing the problem. There is an interaction, which makes the problem worse. If you look at it from the point of view of reward or reinforcement they have a 'negative reinforcement cycle.' It doesn't matter who started it five years ago. The point is that the pattern is that one nags and the other withdraws. More nagging leads to more withdrawing and vice versa. Therefore, it is not usually possible to attribute the blame to one spouse; it is more useful to look at the behaviors that cause and maintain the pattern.

Let us look more closely at the pattern of communication between the clients and the consultant. Initially what usually happens is that both the husband and wife talk to the counselor. They both talk about how terrible the other person is. The initial statements are typically other-directed statements and blaming statements such as, "You should behave differently" and, "If he stopped that then I wouldn't do this." When you stop to think, it is not surprising that they are not talking with each other. If they could talk with each other they probably wouldn't be consulting you. The problem is that they cannot communicate with each other very well.

What is the job of the consultant given this intitial pattern? If the assumption is right, and usually, although not always, it is, the problem lies somewhere between the two of them; it is not exclusively one's problem or the other's problem. What you need to do is to assist them in setting up communication with each other. You must establish the flow of communication between the two of them. There are two strategies that must be employed simultaneously. One is getting the couple talking to each other, and the other is that you must prevent them from talking with you. If you don't set up both of these strategies together the intervention is not going to work. There are some specific techniques you can use in doing this.

Sometimes you can get them to sit so they are facing each other a little bit more than they otherwise would be. In terms of cutting off communication to you, one of the things I find useful is avoiding making eye contact. It is hard to talk to someone who is not making eye contact with you. It is a very good way of discouraging communication, since eye contact is reinforcing.

So, get them talking with each other. This will take some time. It is not necessarily something that will happen right away. The 'other-blaming' ("It's your fault.") statements must be changed to "I'm responsible." statements ("I could do this differently to help. What am I doing to cause and maintain this problem? What can I do differently?")

The consultant in this situation needs several skills different from those required in the intrapersonal situation. One is to keep control of the session; it can get out of hand very easily. In the intrapersonal situation this is not as critical, although you want to keep control of the process to some extent. In the interpersonal situation you have two people who have difficulty in communicating and in resolving conflict. There is bound to be some resistance, and staying in control is critical.

Another important skill in this situation is giving feedback on what you observe in the relationship. How do these clients interact? What are their patterns? In giving feedback a big trap to avoid is blaming one or the other of the couple. Remember that this is a relationship problem between two people. They both have some ownership in it. It is not only one of their faults. It is very, very easy, especially in some situations, to blame one person. For instance, if you have a situation in which one of the parties is quite aggressive and the other is quite silent, it is easy to develop a blaming attitude toward the aggressive one. "You are always talking. Why don't you be quiet and give the other person a chance?" You can acquire a dislike for someone like that very quickly. You have to remember that the silent person contributes to the pattern. It takes 'two to tango.' The silent person's behavior contributes to the original pattern and also shares the responsiblility for reinforcing and maintaining it. They have choice points throughout in terms of whether or not they change the interaction.

The other critical point in terms of giving feedback is to not take sides and to remain neutral. Let me say a little bit more about this because it is hard to do. Being neutral doesn't necessarily mean you never give only one individual negative feedback. At some point in time you may say "Excuse me, you've interrupted. Would you please stop and let the other person continue." You may make an intervention like that, which is obviously taking sides. There is some risk in this but you do it at certain points in a session. The key is that, on balance, the interventions that you make toward individuals must even out. At a given minute in time it may not be an even score card. But try to keep score in your head and by the end of the session, things should even out. If things do not even out in some general way, then you should start asking yourself what is going on. It may be an indication that you are, in fact, taking sides. By taking sides, you often cut down on your effectiveness. However, it may also indicate an impasse is being reached and a more intrapersonal focus may be appropriate.

Assuming that the couple has learned to communicate more effectively and is making progress in resolving the problem, you will want to assist them in the process of setting contracts between themselves with regard to the problem area. By contract, I don't mean something terribly formal. I don't mean you have to bring in a lawyer. But their agreements must be very clear, and it is usually helpful to have them written, especially the first time or two around. Agreement between two people as to what they are going to do, or change, in order to resolve their problem is required. In order to have a meaningful contract there has to be an exchange. Both parties must give something. A contract in which only one person gives something and there is no exchange, isn't a real contract.

In some ways this situation is not unlike labor-management negotiations. The government handles labor negotiations and hires people to mediate between management and unions. One of the things that is critical in these negotiations and also applies at the interpersonal level is that as soon as you get your first concession from one of the parties, make sure it is balanced with a concession from the other one. If not, you are either locked into a situation in which you are not going to get anything else because the one person has stopped at that point in time, or you have a situation in which one person is giving too much and this may be one of the problems in the relationship. Therefore, a balance in terms of concessions is important, particularly at the point when the first concession is made.

One of the points related to contracting is that we have assumed that the couple will resolve their problems. At what point do you work to maintain the system and at what point do you work to change the system by modifying the components within it? Not by changing the behaviors of the people, but by changing the people in the system. At some point you take this course in terms of whether or not couples split. It also occurs in families in terms of the unmanageability and subsequent institutionalization of one member. It also occurs in organizations in terms of laying off or firing individuals. At points then, the objective may not be to salvage the current system but to change it by eliminating parts of it. At that point you may work with them on a contract related to their separation and assist them to do so in as constructive a way as possible.

Boss-subordinate Interpersonal System

The intervention process applied to the boss-subordinate relationship contains mainly similarities to the marital intervention process, with a few differences.

There is a strong tendency for organizations to not deal with these interpersonal issues directly. This is particularly true for boss-subordinate problems, but also applies to interpersonal problems among peers. Usually the problem is ignored and simply continues to fester and cause numerous other problems. People often tolerate incredible amounts of chronic (dull, nagging) pain to avoid acute (stronger) pain of a much shorter duration.

If the organization is aware of the problem it is often in terms of dealing with only one of the people. Someone in the organization often acts as a support for one (or both) of the incumbents, allowing them to vent their concerns about the relationship and the difficulties this is causing.

The irony of this approach is that most of the time it has exactly the opposite effect of what was intended. Clearly the attempt is to help make the situation better. But what in fact happens is that the 'helper' drains off enough of the energy from the person in pain to decrease the necessity of the two people actually getting together and resolving their problem. Now, I am certainly not advocating that it is never appropriate to talk with one of the parties in a painful situation. There are times, when the pain is quite severe or the relationship is beyond saving, when this may be useful. But what I am saying is that these helpers often are not useful and actually help the person to avoid really dealing with the problem.

Assuming that this inappropriate helping either stops or does not occur, what is likely to happen? The next step is often to try to work out the problem by talking to each of the incumbents separately. In some situations which are extremely sensitive or confidential this type of shuttle diplomacy may be acceptable. However, it is seldom the approach of choice for two reasons. In the first place, the problem is not only that the clients have a specific problem but more importantly, that they have trouble communicating with each other. Therefore, they must learn the skills of communicating as well as seeking a solution to the problem. The second point is that it is only when the consultant sees the two parties interacting that an actual assessment can be made, not having to rely so heavily on second hand impressions.

Clearly, then, the intervention of choice is to meet together with the two parties. If this occurs there are several points a consultant needs to keep in mind.

The first is that there is a difference in the power held by the boss and that of the subordinate, and the consultant must be aware of this difference and add appropriate balance. This may involve encouraging the subordinate to participate and trying to keep a fairly balanced (in terms of talking time) exchange going.

A second point is in terms of the communication. Here communication is often much more controlled and unemotional than in a marital counseling situation. This is often due to having less investment in the organizational relationship, and is also due to the typical organizational norms around non-emotional behavior. The purpose of this session is to develop a more acceptable working relationship, not to develop an intimate, emotionally satisfying marriage. I don't think this point can be overemphasized because some consultants 'do their own thing' whatever the situation and whatever the appropriateness. The question that I find most useful to determine the appropriate consultant behavior is "What is the purpose of this session?" If this purpose is to make emotional contact I will intervene differently than if the purpose is to develop a satisfactory organizational relationship.

A third point with regard to this level of intervention is that as much as possible it should be built into the organizational reward system. For instance, it may be possible to use an organizational member as a monitor to determine how the progress is coming. It may be possible to tie the changes into the organizational performance appraisal system. Naturally, not all issues would be appropriate for these processes, but it is important for a consultant to consider.

A final point is that some problems that are presented as interpersonal problems ("Those two are always in conflict; they sure don't like each other.") are actually caused by organizational factors, especially lack of clarity of roles and responsibilities. The conflict may not be caused by any inherent dislike for each other, but rather because particular responsibilities have not been carefully defined and these people feel that they are intruding on each other's territory. This would be an important aspect to determine during the assessment.

NOTES

1. An excellent summary of marital diagnosis approaches can be found in "Tools and techniques for diagnosis in marital and family therapy" by R.E. Cromwell, C.H. Olson and D. Fournier in *Family Process*, 1976, 15(1), 1-50.

QUESTIONS

1. Apply the human systems assessment model to an interpersonal situation in which you are involved.
2. On the basis of this, modify the model to better suit your own situation. Describe your adapted model.
3. Apply the change model to an interpersonal situation in which you are involved.
4. On the basis of this application, modify the model to better suit your own situation. Describe your adapted model.
5. Describe the similarities and differences between intervening in a marital relationship and intervening in a boss-subordinate relationship.
6. List the books or articles you have read and found helpful in this area. Are there any you plan to read? If so, when?

ANNOTATED BIBLIOGRAPHY

Ables, B.S. & Bradsma, J.M. *Therapy for Couples.* San Francisco: Jossey-Bass, 1977.

> A straightforward explanation of the therapy process with couples emphasizing negotiation, communication and re-education. Contains several session excerpts with commentary.

Journal of marriage and family therapy. Formerly the *Journal of marriage and family counseling.* This journal of the American Association for Marriage and Family Therapy provides some excellent articles not only on marital therapy but also on family therapy.

Lederer, W.J. & Jackson, D.D. *The Mirages of Marriage.* New York: Norton, 1968.

> An excellent book that looks first at the false assumptions which are at the root of many marital problems and then presents specific techniques to deal with them.

Walton, R.E. *Interpersonal Peacemaking: Confrontations and third party consultation.* Reading, Mass: Addison-Wesley, 1969.

> A good overview of third-party consultation with some interesting case material.

CHAPTER SIX

Group change

The third level we will consider is the group. We will consider two types of groups, families and organizational work teams, from both the assessment and intervention perspective.

Assessment

In Figure 6:1 we see the consultants' human systems assessment model for the group level. We will consider this model in terms of both families and organizational work teams.

Systems level

The systems level we are considering is the group level.

Systems analysis

Systems analysis involves consideration of input, throughput, output, feedback, boundary, and environment. However, before considering these variables it is useful to consider a diagramatic representation of the two systems. This is contained in Figure 6:2. For the sake of simplicity let us consider a nuclear family with a mother, father, son, and daughter; also consider a work team with a boss and six subordinates. Naturally, both types of systems come in many configurations. The family may be single parent, contain various numbers of children, or be three generational with live-in grandparents. The work team may involve varying numbers of subordinates, subordinates of different ranks (chief accountant, accountants, secretary), or more than one boss (members of the group may have both field and head office reporting relationships).

1) Systems level: group

2) Systems analysis:
   a) Input
   b) Throughput
   c) Output
   d) Feedback
   e) Boundary
   f) Environment

3) Development stage

4) General factors:
   a) Objectives
   b) Structure
   c) Roles
   d) Communication
   e) Reward System
   f) Power
   g) Time
   h) Space

5) Client-consultant relationship

FIGURE 6:1 Consultants' human systems assessment model: group level

a) FAMILY

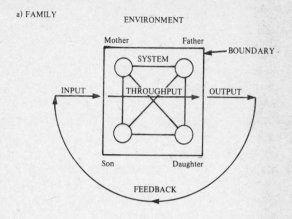

b) ORGANIZATIONAL WORK TEAM

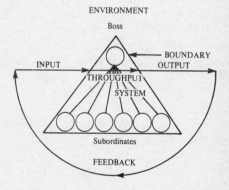

FIGURE 6:2 Two types of groups: family and organizational work team

So while the examples I have chosen certainly do not take into account all possible situations, they will assist in providing the basic analysis required.

One of the first points to be noted about the diagram is that both groups are more complex systems than the ones considered in previous chapters. For instance, in the family system there are four people (intrapersonal level) and six relationships (interpersonal level) (mother-father, mother-son, mother-daughter, father-son, father-daughter, and son-daughter). In the organizational work team there is a boss and six subordinates (intrapersonal level) and twenty-one interpersonal relationships. Therefore, there are considerably more variables than at previous levels.

In terms of input, looking first at the family, this would include: contact with and communication from extended family and friends; money; cultural values; and, government paper work (income tax forms). In terms of the input of a work team, this includes: policies, procedures, and budgets set down by the organization. The input also includes the amount of resources received in terms of people and money, and the expectations that the organization has set for the work team.

What about the throughput of these two systems? What do they do? In terms of the family, one of the main activities is the development, teaching and socialization of children. Other types of activities include leisure activities and developing a supportive, effective, positive environment where people can live, be nurtured and develop. In terms of the work team, two major categories of activities take place. One is related to what the unit is trying to produce. Are they trying to produce a product such as a widget, or are they trying to provide a service such as teaching children. In order to provide the product or service, a work team requires technology. The other category is the maintenance activities that keep the system operating. This includes support and interaction between organizational members.

In terms of output of these two systems, let us first consider the family. One output of a family would be the adolescents or adults sent into the world. Families (and particularly parents) are judged (rightly or wrongly) on this output. This helps to explain why parents are so anxious about their child's behavior. It is easy to say to parents that they have too much invested in their children, and that each of the children must be their own person. This is a good value and philosophy, but is often hard to practice, since parents are, in fact, often judged based on the behavior of those children and the kinds of adults they become. Other types of output of the family include work and activities in the community (running a Scout group or coaching a baseball team). In terms of output of the work team, the major output will be some type of product or service. Often it is difficult for work teams to know exactly what their service or product is and, in particular, how to measure it. In considering teaching as an example, one could say that the output of that process is more mature, responsible and skillful students. They will develop knowledge and ability that will help them in later life, in terms of getting a job and being more fulfilled. How is that measured? How do we know if one teacher is doing a good job and another teacher isn't? This is very difficult to assess.

In terms of feedback, the feedback to a family comes from extended families, schools (particularly if the children aren't behaving), and the community. Feedback often comes if there are serious problems. If there is a poor fit between the output of the family and what the community says the output should be, there may be feedback from the police. For instance, if the community requires law-abiding behavior, and members of a family constantly contravene this requirement, the police, and possibly the courts, may become involved. In terms of the work team, the feedback will come from clients, or even more likely from the organization itself. The organization should have some way of feeding back information to the work team about its performance.

The next aspect of this part of the model is the boundary of both systems. There is a boundary surrounding the work team and there is a boundary surrounding the family. There must be the appropriate balance of elasticity and firmness in the boundary. In terms of the family, there must be enough tightness that there is a family identity and cohesiveness, yet not so much that the family is too focused on itself and lacks contact with the environment. One of the themes related to the boundaries of a family is that there has to be a balance between differentiation and integration. Family members need to be integrated into a family unit to the extent that they are part of it, that there is some satisfaction and support from it. On the other hand they need to be separate enough (differentiated) to develop their unique personalities. This is particularly important as children are growing up. They have different needs to differentiate from the family at different developmental stages. What is an appropriate closeness to a family for a 6-year-old is, in most cases, not an appropriate closeness to a family for a 15-year-old.

The same general points pertain to the work team. There has to be enough of a boundary around the work team to create a cohesiveness, an identity, and an ability to work together. On the other hand, there has to be some separateness and freedom for people to function within that unit. One of the key questions pertaining to work teams in organizations is: "How functionally related are they? How much do they need each other in terms of the tasks they do?" In point of fact, often work teams are not very interdependent or functionally related. For example, each teacher in the English department in a high school has a specific class that is taught in a particular way. The teachers have little contact with each other and usually do not need each other. The absence of a functional relationship minimizes the chances of developing a cohesive group. So the functional interrelationship of a team is important in determining how successful one can be in building a team and whether or not building a team is a useful strategy.

The final aspect of the model is the environment of these two systems. For the family system, important parts of the environment include the extended family (grandparents of the children); the school (particularly with school-age children); the community; the work situation; the government; and, the municipality in which the family lives. Another important part of the environment for a family, which is very pervasive and vague, is the social and cultural norms of a particular society. In terms of the environment of the work team, the most significant part of it is the rest of the organization of which the team is a part. The activities of the rest of the organization have a tremendous effect on the work team. Other important parts of the environment of the work team include the government and other organizations with which they relate (suppliers, clients, competitors). Another part of the work team environment is the families of the team members. We can begin to see the connection between these two systems. They are parts of each other's environment. They have some very direct impact on each other.

Developmental stage

The next point in our model is the developmental stage of the group. The developmental stage of a family is usually defined by the developmental stages of the individuals in it, particularly of the children. While there is no set developmental pattern, some of the significant stages include: the birth of the first child; the birth of additional children; the developmental stages of the children; and, finally, their departure from home. The assessment of the stages of a work team is much more difficult since their membership is constantly shifting. In this sense they are less stable than a family. This is particularly true in times of high turnover, and is accentuated when the boss is new. While there is little data on the developmental stages of a work team there is some data on the development of stranger-groups, which may be useful to the consultant.[1]

General Factors

The next part of the model involves consideration of eight general factors. These include: objectives, structure, roles, communication, reward system, power, time, and space.

The first of these is the objectives of the group. What is that group trying to accomplish? What are its priorities? In a family with young children the objectives are determined by the parents although they are largely based upon the children's needs. However, as the children get older, a more mutual decision-making process usually takes place. Some of the questions related to objectives include: "How much closeness do we want? What are our objectives in terms of the amount of warmth and kind of nurturence we are going to give the children? How much autonomy do we want to give the children to develop on their own? How much personal leisure time do we want, away from the children? What are our objectives as a family in terms of money? Are we prepared to say that we don't want quite as much money and we want to have more time together? What are our objectives in terms of activities within the community of which we are a part? Is it acceptable to have separate friends, or should we try to cultivate joint friends?" These are examples of the kinds of questions that affect families and yet are very seldom discussed openly. And the fact that they aren't discussed often leads to problems.

In terms of the objectives of the work team, there is one primary objective of the work team and that is to provide a good service or product. Again, there are many ways in which this could be defined. It could be in terms of the quality of the service or product or in terms of the number of clients, or in terms of the level of profitability. One of the differences between government and business is that business has easier measures of outcome. In business there are many financial measures. Accounting firms, for example, often have excellent measures. They can assess staff on many factors including total hours, productive hours, gross billings, uncollected billings, new clients, and lost clients. They can, therefore, set some very specific and relevant objectives.

A secondary objective of a work team is creating an environment which will attract, retain and satisfy people. This is referred to as a maintenance function and is often critical to meeting the primary objective.

The next variable is structure. In the structure of the family, one finds a hierarchical system with the parents at the top of the system and the children below. The structure is often discussed in terms of communication and power. Essentially, there are two important subsystems in a family. There is a parent subsystem of the mother and father; this is also the spouse subsystem. They are husband and wife as well as mother and father, and must maintain these dual roles. Then there is a children, or sibling, subsystem. A breakdown of the subsystems often leads to serious problems. This is particularly true for the mother-father subsystem. If it is not cohesive enough, if mother and father start getting too close to son and daughter, and if the generation gap isn't sufficiently clear and distinct, there may be confusion as to who is the parent in the family and who is the child. Often children are put into a situation of having to take sides and be a judge in a parental fight; this places a tremendous stress on the children.

Continuing with the concept of structure, I would like to shift over to look at the structure of a work team. The structure here is different in that there are at least two distinct levels. In fact, there may be three levels in a work team when it includes support staff such as secretaries. Often this support person's relationship to the person in charge of the department and to the other people is not very clear. Is that support person responsible to everyone in the department or just to the person in charge of the department? In situations where there are two levels in a work team, the person in charge of a unit and the subordinates working for that person, the major subsystem would be the subordinate subsystem.

The next area to consider is the roles that people play in these situations. In a family, there are several different roles each member plays. The man is both a husband and a father, the woman both a wife and mother. The children are children relative to the parents but also siblings in relation to each other. So there are child-child relationships, parent-child relationships and parent-parent relationships. The point here is that people have to be clear in a family about each others' roles. They have to work out potential incompatabilities in those roles. It is often the 'small issues' (who cleans the house, who takes out the garbage, who helps the children with homework) that lead to major problems.

Role problems can also occur in work teams. What are the roles and how do they interrelate? Are the roles clear? Do people know what they are supposed to be doing? Also, one of the important role aspects that needs to be worked out in a work team is the kind of authority relationship the person in charge is going to have with the other people. This varies tremendously from situation to situation, all the way from very autocratic to very democratic.

In terms of communication, different aspects are critical for families and organizational groups. For instance, in families it is important to consider the congruence of messages sent. In most troubled families (and in many normal families to a lesser degree) mixed messages are sent. At more simple levels this can cause confusion and discomfort. At more extreme levels we can have a double bind (where an individual is trapped and cannot perform successfully); it is hypothesized that this is one of the causes of schizophrenia.[2]

In work groups we are more concerned with the flow of information within the group. Basically, we need to consider whether group members have sufficient information to make decisions. Furthermore we are concerned with the quantity of information, wanting to determine that while all relevant information is present, there is no serious redundancy or overlap.

In terms of the reward system, the question for both of these systems is simply, "Is the system rewarding the kind of behavior it really wants?" And often the kind of behavior that a system states officially that it wants, and the kind that it demonstrates that it wants in its actions are quite different. An example would be with young children. Parents will sometimes say, "My child is acting out and having tantrums, and I really don't like that. I want the tantrums to stop." You observe what occurs in the family around the child's tantrums. First of all, the parents pay attention when the child is having a tantrum, so just in terms of attention there is a tendency to reinforce the behavior. But then you look more closely and notice that when this happens at least one of the parents smiles and implicitly says, "Isn't that cute." There is some additional reinforcement to maintain the behavior. So, on the one level, the parents are saying they don't like this behavior and want it to stop. But, on the other hand they are doing things to maintain it. So the reward system is incompatible with the behavior they say they want. They need to be clear about what behavior they really want and then make the reward system consistent with that.

The same is true for work groups in that many problems are caused by inconsistent reward system practices. On the one hand there is a statement that they want high quality and good results. On the other hand, the system makes it very difficult to get rid of people who are not performing well. So, the system really rewards longevity rather than performance. If a person can survive for three to five years then that person has got it made. The only way that they are going to get rid of anyone is if someone does something illegal or immoral. The reward system isn't consistent with the statement of desired behaviors. The other thing that often happens in organizational groups is that they say they want people to be individualistic, innovative, keen, and full of new ideas. When one looks at what happens to new suggestions, and what happens to people who take risks and do something new that does not work out perfectly it becomes clear that the system doesn't support this kind of behavior. There is an incongruence. And that has to change in order for the system to operate effectively.

The next dimension is power, and in terms of power, there are power differentials in both families and work teams. In families parents have more power than children, since they have more control over resources. How parents deal with this power varies from family to family. This power differential decreases as the children get older. However, small children also have power in the family, albeit a different type of power. Children can often get their own way by acting out for extended periods of time, knowing that the parents will get tired and give in (parents cancel plan to go out for fear that child will have a tantrum).

Power is also an important concept in work teams. Of course, the power of a work team is limited to start with. The person in charge of the unit doesn't have full power over that unit, and has to work within parameters that are laid down from the outside. One of the causes of frustration in organizations is making the false assumption that the person in charge of a unit can change things. The person in charge may have relatively more power than the subordinates but often not sufficient power to make significant changes.

In terms of time orientation, there is a tendency for families at different developmental stages to have different time focuses. Very early there is often a future orientation, which changes to a present orientation, which sometimes goes back to a past orientation. Of course, this is a broad generalization and it doesn't always apply. However, early in the life of a couple there is planning for children and the future. Then dealing with the family in the present requires the most energy. After the children leave there is a tendency to look back on the early stages. The practice in our society of taking pictures is a good example of developing this past orientation.

The most important time orientation for a work team is often the future. The past doesn't become quite as important for a work team. The future orientation becomes important in terms of what is going to be done, and plans are made in advance. The government often uses a five-year budgetary planning cycle. So the planning in terms of the budget cycle is long term and forces a future orientation, especially for those at the upper levels of departments. At the lower levels there may be more of a tendency to have a present orientation.

The next area to consider briefly is space. The assessment of space can often provide very good clues about what is happening in a group and what potential problems are. For instance, the ways in which members of a family decorate their house, organize their house, set up their living and sleeping areas, and allocate space to people is a very good indication of their values, their priorities and kinds of behavior one might expect as a result of the space usage. An example would be a family with small children that has very nice furniture throughout the house. Every time the children try to do something, the parents say "Don't do that, it will make a mess." There is nowhere for the children to make a mess, to play, to be creative. Clearly the space allocation is inappropriate. Another example is a situation in which the children are always fighting and you find out that there are three children in one bedroom. There is a bunkbed on one wall and a single bed on the other wall. One intervention would be to try to divide up the space more effectively to give each child some private space.

In terms of the work team, you can often observe their space and learn a lot about them. What kinds of work space do people have? Who has the nicest work space? Who has the carpets? Where is this work team located relative to the other work teams within an organization.

Client-consultant relationship

The client-consultant relationship is diagrammed in Figure 6:3. It becomes obvious from considering the diagram how much more complex the interaction can be at the group level. It is important to recognize that each member of the group (be it a family or an organizational work team) has a relationship with every other member as well as with the consultant. In a family example, with four family members, the interaction is a fairly complex one; in the work team example, with seven group members, the complexity of interaction increases significantly. Clearly the consultant needs to be aware of a variety of interaction, must be able to assess a complex system, and requires many intervention strategies.

Before moving on to the intervention discussion, we must consider the assessment of the change potential in terms of motivation, skill, and power. Often in group situations the motivation varies considerably among the various group members. Some will be fairly committed to a change process and others will not, in accordance with their view of the potential benefits and costs of the process. Therefore, one of the important considerations is whether or not there is sufficient power-backing for the change process. In particular, it is critical that the power figures in the group (the parents in the family situation and the boss in a work team situation) are supportive of the process. Often in families you will find that one parent (usually the mother) is supportive of the change process while the other (usually the father) is more ambivalent. This leads to strategic decisions of how to get the ambivalent parent more involved.

In terms of skills, in the group situation one of the key factors is how the group shares information and makes decisions. In the family situation, one of the critical issues is how the family resolves conflict. Often the presence of a family in a family-therapy situation is an indication of the inability to resolve conflict and this, therefore, becomes a major focus of the change process.

Intervention

I would like to shift here and concentrate more specifically on the change process. How is the change process different at the group level? Probably the best way to understand the process would be to take an example of a family. The basic difference is that there is no interest in directly changing one person or even changing two

a) CONSULTANT RELATIONSHIP WITH FAMILY

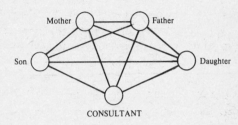

b) CONSULTANT RELATIONSHIP WITH
ORGANIZATIONAL WORK TEAM

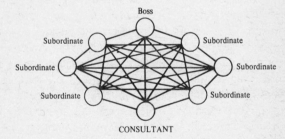

FIGURE 6:3 Consultant relationship with family and organizational work
team

people. The interest is in changing a group. In order to change a group sometimes interventions must be made which are aimed at one person (intrapersonal) or two people (interpersonal). But, interventions aimed at changing the group also must be made. We now have three potential levels of intervention.

Let me give you an example. In a family interaction one person says, "I don't like that idea." A second person in a family says, "Why don't you shut up!" This brief interaction could be handled at three different levels. It could be handled at an intrapersonal level, where you would say to one person, "You seem quite angry, from that comment; what is going on?" You would focus on that person and you would work at helping that person to gain insight or to change in some way. However, your intervention could also be focused at an interpersonal level. You could say "I see that the two of you are at it again. What is going on between the two of you?" So, you have a relationship focus. Or, finally, it could be focused at a group level. You could say, "Whenever anyone in this group comes up with an idea, it is always shot down. You don't seem to be able, as a group, to get any momentum going in making decisions and in doing things." What you do in this case is to focus the responsibility on all of the people in the group; you make a group level intervention. In the first response you are focusing on one person. In the second response you are focusing on two people, and in the third response you are focusing on the group. What one usually finds is that consultants are not very effective at making group level interventions. Our training focuses very much on making individual interventions. We have considerable training and experience in focusing on one person. We have less training and experience in making a relationship or interpersonal level intervention. We have even less training and experience in making a group level intervention. Therefore, in terms of skill development, it is often necessary to focus on these latter two areas in particular since they are often the most neglected.

In order to effectively change a group it is important to accurately assess the causes of the problems and relate the intervention to them. Let me give you an example. I was working with a particular family when I was in training as a family therapist. The family consisted of a mother, a father and two sons aged ten and fourteen. The mother was quite aggressive and attacking. The father was very passive and withdrawn. He just didn't make contact; he was there but he wasn't there. The initial presenting problem involved one of the sons. He was very withdrawn at school, his marks seemed to be dropping, and he had few friends. It was a pattern that had been building over a period of time. The other sibling, in the initial stages of therapy, seemed not to have any problems. They came to the first session and the mother started talking and was very easy to engage. She talked about the family, her disappointment in the son, and her difficulties with her husband. I focused on her and asked her how she felt about various aspects of her life. Father was sitting back there, pleased as punch because he didn't have to deal with his wife at all since I was doing it. We were going along like this through a couple of sessions and I believed that this woman was really gaining some insight into herself, and that I was being very helpful. These sessions were all videotaped and I went to meet with my supervisor one day and went over a tape with him. He said to me, "What do you think is the major problem in the family?" I thought about it for a minute and then I said, "The initial problem they talked about was the son being quiet. But I don't think that is the major problem. I think the major problem is that the mother and father can't communicate and there is a real conflict there and the son's way of dealing with it is to withdraw. He is using that withdrawal behavior at home and also using it at school. So, I think the root of the problem is really the parent's relationship." He said, "Yes, I think that is right. That is a good assessment," and then he looked at me and said, "And how are you contributing to their problem?" I was somewhat taken aback and had to think about that for a few minutes. I was contributing to their problem because I wasn't helping them to talk, which was really first of all their major problem and secondly the factor that was pushing out the son and causing him to withdraw. I thought I was being very helpful doing that individual counseling, when in point of fact I wasn't at all. I wasn't helping them with their major problem. What I needed to do at that point was to work with the mother and father at communicating with each other. This meant giving father some support, and toning mother down at the same time. While the process was a difficult one it had a positive effect on their family system.

The pattern of communicating is more complex at the group level. At the intrapersonal level we focused on the sending and receiving of messages. At the interpersonal level we looked at the pattern of interaction between two people and how they were affecting each other. At the group level we encounter a transactional pattern for the first time. A transaction is a pattern of communication involving three or more people, and is more difficult to observe and assess than the previous two. An example of a transaction is a family situation in which the mother will say something, the father will get angry at her, and their child then has a tantrum. The three behaviors are related in a sequence and form a recurring pattern. Often groups fail to see the pattern (fail to see that the child's tantrum is related to parent's anger).

The first step in dealing with transactions is recognizing them. This can be assisted by looking for recurring patterns such as the one just described.

The second step is to determine whether or not the pattern is dysfunctional. There are some transactional patterns that are positive and don't require change. The third step is, if the pattern is dysfunctional, to develop strategies to change it. There are several alternatives to consider. First, have the family become aware that the pattern is in fact occurring and develop the ability to recognize it. Second, work with them at developing new behavior to interrupt the pattern, subsequently developing a new one to replace it.

While up to this point we have considered the family, the comments also apply to work teams. As well, there is another area we should discuss which has more application to work teams than to families. That is the ability to conduct an effective group meeting.3 Families also need to be able to meet effectively but on a more informal basis.

There are many basic points important to conducting successful meetings. The first is that it is important to have an agenda. Team members should contribute so that the agenda reflects the needs of all the group members and they will know in advance about any issues for which they need to prepare. One of the problems with meetings occurs when groups are expected to make decisions, but there is no prior knowledge about what those decisions might be and the members cannot adequately prepare. The agenda should not only indicate the items that will be discussed but also the amount of time that will be allocated to each item. The reason time allotment is important is that what typically happens is there are ten items on an agenda and there are sixty minutes to cover them, the first three items take forty-five minutes and the other seven receive only fifteen munutes. Needless to say, this leads to many poor-quality decisions. It is also useful to specify on the agenda whether an item is included for information purposes only or for purposes of decision making. What often happens is that an information item will be discussed ad infinitum and at the end of the discussion everyone will be frustrated because they won't know what they are supposed to do with the item. An information item should only take a couple of minutes to complete.

A further point, which is obvious but unfortunately often over-looked, is that the agenda items should be relevant for the group that is meeting. For instance, in a staff meeting, it may be appropri-ate as an informational point for the head of one of the departments to take a few minutes to inform others about major developments in this area. But it is not relevant to discuss them at length if that is not the mandate of the whole group.

In order to conduct a successful meeting two obvious roles must be filled and a third one is important. The two obvious roles are a chair person and a secretary. The chair person basically runs the meeting, keeps things on track and keeps the group focused. The whole group has some responsibility for this, but the chair person has primary responsibility. A secretary records any decisions or out-comes of the meeting in the minutes. The third important role is that of timekeeper. Particularly when a group is learning the skill of keeping within time boundaries, the role of timekeeper is impor-tant.

Another important point is to have some time at the end of the meeting to discuss the effectiveness of the meeting and to deter-mine the factors that contributed to or detracted from its success. I refer to this as 'process time.' One of the incomprehensible facts about our society is that we spend a great deal of time in meetings, yet receive virtually no special training for this. There is no feedback as to how effective we are. This process time builds a feedback link in the group so that it can assess itself and hopefully develop more effective skills.

Two other factors with regard to the process of the meeting should be considered. One is that it is important to know how a group makes decisions. What often happens in meetings is that there is a pressure toward making decisions through concensus. However, this approach only works well if the group has unlimited time. What usually happens is that the group is not making decisions by concensus, but using some sham of that approach. Examples of the sham are when the chair person says, after the discussion has taken place for ten or fifteen minutes, "Well, I think we all agree to the decision now; let's move on to the next item." That is not con-census. What you have in that situation is people who disagree but don't say anything. One of the clues to a faulty decision-making process occurs when the group thinks it has made a decision but fifteen minutes later someone comes back and says, "You know that issue we were discussing earlier; I really wanted to say this about it," and the whole issue opens up again.

The final point is in terms of the recorded outcome of the meeting, the minutes. Most organizational meetings should have minutes, but the way most minutes are compiled is absolutely useless unless you happen to be a social historian who is interested in the social development of the group over an extended period. The minutes are very chatty and are not terribly relevant. It seems to me that there are really only two areas that need to be covered in minutes. One is decisions that the group makes around policies and procedures, and the second area covers any action plans that the group makes. An action plan is a plan that lists what is going to be done, who is going to do it, when it is going to be done, and a check person. The job of the check person is to write on a calendar pad the date that the item is to be completed, who is to have done it and what is supposed to have been done. And on that date, if the check person has received the information already, nothing is done. In a good organization, the check person is very inactive. However, if nothing has been received, it is the check person's responsibility to go to the other person and find out why.

NOTES

1. One of the more recent articles is "Sequential stages of development in sensitivity training groups" by D. Lundgren and D.J. Knight in *The Journal of Applied Behavior Science* (1978, 4(2) 204-22). While discussing a specific research project it also cites other sources in the group development area.
2. A summary of the double-bind theory can be found in "A review of double-bind theory" by P. Watzlawick in a book edited by D. Jackson, *Communication, Family and Marriage* (Palo Alto: Science and Behavior Books, 1968).
3. A useful book on group meetings is *Making Meetings Work* by Leland Bradford (Eads, Ca.: University Associates, 1976).

112

QUESTIONS

1. Use the consultant's human systems assessment model (Figure 6:1) to describe a family with which you are familiar.
2. Use the assessment model to describe a work group with which you are familiar.
3. Describe the similarities and differences between families and work groups in terms of assessment.
4. Assess yourself on the three new intervention strategies presented in this chapter (group level interventions, transactions, group meetings).
5. What are the similarities and differences in intervening with families and work groups?
6. What books have you read that are helpful at the group level? What books do you plan to read?.

ANNOTATED BIBLIOGRAPHY

A) Family Literature

Family Process

This is one of the best available journals in the family change area. Provides information about approaches and techniques for working with families.

Foley, V. *An Introduction to Family Therapy.* New York: Grune & Stratton, 1974.

A very good introduction to family therapy covering the seminal ideas (double bind, pseudomutuality and pseudohostility, schism and skew, mystification and general system theory) and the seminal theorists, Ackerman, Bowen, Jackson, Haley & Satir.

Haley, J., ed. *Changing Families.* New York: Grune & Stratton, 1971.

A book of readings that presents a wide range of views and approaches in the family therapy area.

Haley, J. & Hoffman, L. *Techniques of Family Therapy.* New York: Basic Books, 1967.

A unique and valuable book in that transcripts are presented of five cases and the therapists explain their rationale for various approaches at different points in time.

Kantor, D. & Lehr, W. *Inside the Family.* San Francisco: Jossey-Bass, 1975.

While this book is about the organization and behavior of the family rather than the change process per se, it is one of the most useful and original works available for understanding how the family operates.

Minuchin, S. *Families and Family Therapy.* Cambridge: Harvard University Press, 1974.

One of the most integrated books in the area presents Minuchin's structural approach. Includes some transcripts and much rich learning.

Speck, R. & Attneave, C. L. *Family Networks.* New York: Pantheon Books, 1973.

An approach is outlined to treating family crises by mobilizing the family's network. An original approach that contrasts sharply with the tendency to consider only the internal workings of the family.

B) Group Literature

Benne, K.D., Bradford, L.P., Gibb, J.R. & Lippitt, R.O., eds. *The Laboratory Method of Changing and Learning.* Palo Alto: Science and Behavior Books, 1975.

A revised edition of the classic on laboratory training, this book contains many excellent articles that also consider the individual, organization and community levels of change.

Group and Organization Studies
   A more recent journal containing some good articles on group and organization change.
Journal of Applied Behavioral Science
   Published by N.T.L. Institute, this excellent journal contains mainly applied articles on change in groups and organizations.
Schien, E.H. & Bennis, W.G. *Personal and Organizational Change Through Group Methods.* New York: Wiley, 1965.
   While some of the articles are dated, this classic still contains much useful information about laboratory training.
Yalom, I.D. *The Theory and Practice of Group Psychotherapy.* New York: Basic Books, 1970.
   While this book tends to look at individual change through the group process there are many interesting observations on group functioning and process.

CHAPTER SEVEN

Intergroup change

There are many examples of the intergroup systems level. These include the relations between two departments or units in an organization, two families in a neighborhood, two informal groups in a school, the police and a certain group in a community, and a labor and management group. The group, therefore, may be formal, such as an organizational department, or informal, such as members of a neighborhood gang.

In terms of our discussion of the intergroup level we will use as an example the relationship between two formal groups. We will consider both the assessment and intervention aspects.

Assessment

In Figure 7:1 we see the consultants' human systems assessment model. The model involves specifying the systems level, completing a systems analysis, determining the developmental stage, considering several general factors and looking at the client-consultant relationship.

Before considering these factors it would be useful to look at a diagramatic representation of an intergroup relationship. This is shown in Figure 7:2. We are considering two departments of an organization.[1] We see that there is an interaction between the two groups. It is important to note that the interaction can occur between any levels of the systems. For instance, the two bosses may meet to discuss mutual policy issues and the subordinates may work together on particular projects or have contact to share information.

Let us now consider the five factors of the model and the assessment of change potential.

1) Systems level: intergroup

2) Systems analysis:
   a) Input
   b) Throughput
   c) Output
   d) Feedback
   e) Boundary
   f) Environment

3) Developmental stage

4) General factors:
   a) Objectives
   b) Structure
   c) Roles
   d) Communication
   e) Reward system
   f) Power
   g) Time
   h) Space

5) Client-consultant relationship

FIGURE 7:1 Consultants' human systems assessment model: intergroup level

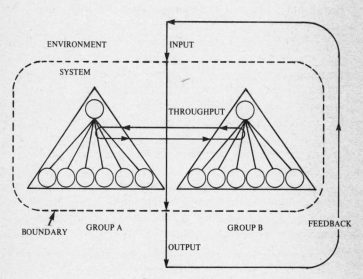

FIGURE 7:2 Intergroup human system

Systems level

The systems level under consideration is the intergroup level.

Systems analysis

The systems analysis involves looking at input, throughput, output, feedback, boundary, and environment.

The input into the intergroup system will include any incoming information or actions which affect the groups. This includes resources and values from the environment.

The throughput of the intergroup system is the interaction between the two groups. As previously mentioned, this can take place at any levels between the groups. The throughput involves all interaction between the two groups and is particularly concerned with the communication and negotiation that takes place between them.

The output of the intergroup system involves any communication or action coming from their joint interaction. It may involve joint actions (each group sending representatives to a mutually developed and controled work group) or words (sending a joint communique indicating agreement or disagreement on certain points).

The feedback that the intergroup system receives comes from various parts of the environment. This is a particularly important aspect of considering the intergroup relationship, since the feedback is often distorted. This becomes a particular problem when there is some animosity between the groups since there is a tendency for the groups to selectively attend to negative aspects of the feedback. For instance, if there is a conflict between the sales and production departments of an organization, any customer complaints to the sales staff about the quality of a particular piece of equipment could be used to confirm the sales staff's bias that the production department is ineffective (not noting that it is only one customer in a hundred that is complaining).

The boundary between the groups and the environment (as indicated in Figure 7:2) is not very solid. In most cases the intergroup relationship is less tight and less cohesive than at the interpersonal levels we have considered. This is particularly true when the groups have more difference than similarity in their environments.

The last factor to consider is the environment. It is important to note that the environment of the two groups are partially overlapping and partially unique to only one group. For instance, when one considers sales and production groups, the environments of both groups include the upper levels of the company (in terms of policy and directives). On the other hand, parts of the environment only affect one group directly. The customers are directly part of the sales group's environment and maintenance engineers (to maintain production equipment) are only part of the production group's environment.

Developmental stage

The developmental stages of intergroup relations are not well defined. However, even if it is not possible to determine the developmental stage, it is important to be aware of how previous events affect the current situation. For instance, if two departments have a history of conflict it is likely that they have begun to attend selectively to their environment to find the confirming information that the other party is untrustworthy.

General factors

There are eight general factors to consider. These include objectives, structure, roles, communication, reward system, power, time, and space.

In terms of objectives, it is important to remember that the two groups have different objectives. It is very important to determine the similarities and differences between the objectives of the two groups. For instance, in our example of sales and production groups, the primary objective of the sales group is to sell as much as possible; the primary objective of the production department is to produce a high quality product that will not malfunction. So the primary objective is different for each and has the potential for conflict (the sales department has a rush order and needs additional supplies within two days; the production department is reluctant because they won't be able to do as thorough an inspection and will be required to pay overtime to the production people and, therefore, go over budget). It is necessary in this case to look for an overriding objective (best service to the customer) to assist in reaching the best decision.

The next factor, structure, involves consideration of both the intragroup and the intergroup structures. Both groups should have strong internal structures since this leads to more effectively managing any commitments that emerge from discussions. An implication of the intergroup structure is that since both groups have more than one level, it is important to determine how they interact at the various levels.

In terms of roles, one of the roles that is often built into this situation is the adversarial role. The groups are on opposite sides. This becomes particularly important for an individual representing a group. The individual's title may be 'negotiator,' and there is a certain role conflict. On the one hand an equitable outcome must be reached with the other negotiator. On the other hand, the major role is to represent the group's interests. When this role conflict is clear, one can better appreciate the difficulties in resolving intergroup conflicts.

The next factor, communication, is often inadequate in two ways. In the first place there is not sufficient communication between the groups. Often in an adversarial situation, withholding of information is one of the strategies used to maintain and enhance power. Second, there is a strong tendency for the messages to be filtered. With an adversary we tend to only believe the negative things said about them, and also tend to read negative intentions into their words and actions.

The reward or motivation system is important to understand since often the groups perceive themselves as getting more reward for not resolving a conflict than for resolving it. There may be some loss of status (real or perceived) in reaching a mutual accommodation. Obviously, one of the things a consultant needs to be in a position to do is to affect the reward system so that there is more benefit in reaching a mutual accommodation than in not doing so. For instance, the funding of the two groups could be partially contingent upon their resolving a conflict or successfully managing a joint project.

The dimension of power is extremely important in these situations. Especially when there is an overt conflict between two groups, it is important to be able to assess their power bases. The analysis would include the power base of the groups (which people or groups support them and would aid them) and their strengths and weaknesses. In any tactical manoeuvering between two groups each will seek to attack the other groups' weakness with their strength.

In terms of time, it is important to assess the groups from an historical perspective (how did the problems first develop, what solutions have been attempted in the past); a present perspective (describing their current interaction); and a future perspective (a likely

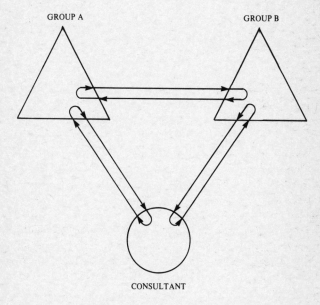

FIGURE 7:3 Consultant relationship with intergroup system

future scenario of their relationship). It is also useful to determine how much time the groups spend together and in what manner.

In terms of space, the two systems will usually occupy different spaces. They may come together at points on one or the other's space. If they do have common space an assessment of how it is used and maintained may give some indication as to the nature of the relationship.

Client-consultant relationship

The client-consultant relationship is diagrammed in Figure 7:3. As is shown, both groups have a relationship with each other and the consultant has a relationship with each of the groups. However, the actual relationship is more complicated, since the members of each group also have relationships with each other. Therefore this is a very complex network of interrelationships in which the consultant is involved.

Before moving on to the intervention we will consider the change potential, in terms of motivation, skill, and power, for each of the groups. More likely than not you will find a situation where the motivation of one of the groups is quite high but the motivation of the other group is relatively low. In a situation such as this it would be necessary first to raise the motivation of the lower group to an acceptable level. My experience has been that most formal groups, particularly those in organizations, have sufficient skill to resolve most problem situations. This tends to be less true for informal groups, particularly in certain types of community development work. In this latter case it is often necessary first to raise skill levels. In terms of power, the groups may or may not have sufficient power to resolve critical issues. In situations where they do not, it would be necessary first to increase the power base of the two groups and/or get support from the appropriate power sources.

Intervention

Before beginning the intervention phase it is necessary to do a thorough assessment. While we have emphasized the assessment at all levels up to now, it becomes increasingly important at the intergroup and more complex levels. With a thorough assessment it often becomes quite apparent what the intervention should involve. However, particularly in a serious conflict situation between the two groups, the assessment had better be correct, because there may not be a second chance to intervene.

There are many clues from the assessment as to possible intervention targets. First of all, it may be possible to tighten up the boundary around the two groups. This would involve making them more interdependent and increasing their degree of interaction. An example may be having them jointly work out production schedules and sales quotas.

A second intervention point from the systems analysis is to increase the pressure from the environment for certain kinds of actions. For instance, if customers banded together and started making certain demands, this would certainly have an impact on the nature of the relationship between the two groups and would force closer cooperation.

A third strategy is to work on making the objectives more compatible. For instance, if both the sales and production departments had more identity with overall customer service objectives, the internal conflict would lessen.

A point related to structure is that it is important to determine that both groups have enough internal strength. This seems paradoxical since the conventional wisdom is often that one group should be weak. The problem is that when this occurs the weak group is often unable to enforce agreements. An example would be a weak union whose members have frequent wildcat strikes.

In terms of communication, the consultant can often play a significant role in improving the quality of communication by breaking down misperceptions and stereotypes. This is often one of the most important functions.

The reward system is also important for the consultant since there must be sufficient rewards for positive change to counter any costs of the change. It is clear that groups will not change unless it is in their own best interests to do so. It is important to note that it is sometimes possible to include the guarantee of no sanction in the reward system. For instance, the police sometimes drop a charge against someone in exchange for evidence.

Power is a key concept for consultants, not only in terms of understanding the power base of pairs of groups, but perhaps more importantly in understanding their own power base. If consultants can draw part of their power from sources that have power over pairs of groups (the general manager to whom the sales manager and production manager report) they will be in much stronger positions.

In terms of time, one of the strategies of the consultant is to get the groups to spend less time on the past (both often have a high investment in citing past grievances) and more time on the future (in terms of directions that can be of mutual benefit).

In terms of space, a critical strategy is for the consultant to make sure that the groups meet on neutral territory. It would, in most cases, be inappropriate to meet on the territory of one or other of the groups.

Up to this point in time we have talked about the groups getting together. While this often happens, especially in situations where the groups are small, it is also often the case that the representatives of the groups (the sales and production managers) will meet. This creates an interesting situation because while the two heads are under some pressure to arrive at an understanding or resolution, they are also under pressure to defend their own groups' rights. The key factor in determining where their primary allegiance is comes from determining who is paying them. In an organizational situation the managers generally have primary allegiance to the organization. However, in a union situation, where the representative was elected by this group to represent them (and where this person can get thrown out of office if perceived not to be doing an adequate job), the tendency is to more strongly represent the group.

NOTES

1. An interesting article on interdepartmental conflicts is "Third party roles in interdepartmental conflict" by R.E. Walton in *Industrial Relations*, 1967, 7, 29-43.

126

QUESTIONS

1. Apply the consultants' human systems assessment model to an intergroup situation with which you are familiar.
2. On the basis of this modify the model to better suit your own situation. Describe your adapted model.
3. Apply elements of the intervention discussion to a situation in which you are involved. Which would have the greatest impact? Why?

ANNOTATED BIBLIOGRAPHY

Blake, R.R., Shepard, H.A. & Mouton, J.S. *Managing Intergroup Conflict in Industry*. Houston: Gulf, 1964.

CHAPTER EIGHT

Organization change

In this chapter we will consider the organization human systems level. We will consider the organization from both the assessment and intervention perspectives.

Assessment

In Figure 8:1 we have the consultants' human systems assessment model for the organization level. The model consists of looking at the human systems level, completing a systems analysis, considering the developmental stage, analyzing eight general factors, and considering the client-consultant relationship.

However, before considering these factors we will look at the diagrammatic representation of the organization found in Figure 8:2. We have created a simple organization involving three levels and a total of nine organizational members. While most organizations are much more complex than this, our example will serve to highlight some of the basic factors that must be taken into account in dealing with organizations.

It should be noted that the input and output of an organization occur at different points in the organization, not simply at one point, as the arrows indicate. For instance, the president of the organization may send and receive information to and from competitors and government representatives. The middle managers may have contact with major suppliers and major customers. The front line staff may have primary contact with the service companies (servicing their equipment) and potential customers.

Let us now consider the five-part human systems assessment model and also the assessment of change potential.

130

1) Systems level: organization

2) Systems analysis:
   a) Input
   b) Throughput
   c) Output
   d) Feedback
   e) Boundary
   f) Environment

3) Development stage

4) General factors:
   a) Objectives
   b) Structure
   c) Roles
   d) Communication
   e) Reward system
   f) Power
   g) Time
   h) Space

5) Client-consultant relationship

FIGURE 8:1 Consultants' human systems assessment model: organization level

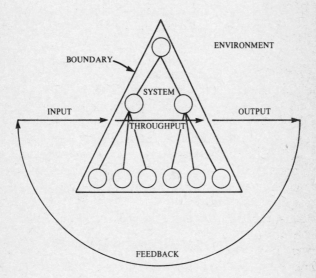

FIGURE 8:2 Organization human system

Systems level

The human systems level we are considering is the organization.

Systems analysis

The systems analysis consists of looking at the input, throughput, output, feedback, boundary, and environment of the organization.

The input of an organization tends to be money (from investors or government support), people (one of the keys of an organization is the ability to locate, attract and retain competent staff), physical equipment (this is particularly critical for organizations that are highly industrialized) and raw materials (many organizations transform raw material such as leather into a product such as shoes). An organization requires sufficient high quality input or resources in order to survive. The lack of any of these factors could be sufficient to cause the demise of an organization.

The throughput of the organization relates primarily to technology and social systems. I use the word technology very loosely. At times technology can be very sophisticated, such as an assembly line of a new plant. At times technology can be the skills of a teacher or a social worker, including ideas, approaches and techniques. However, an effective technology is not sufficient for a successful throughput function. As well, it is necessary to attend to the needs of the staff and the way they relate to technology.[1] So it is necessary to maintain the social system as well as the technological system. Both are important for organizations to function effectively.

The output of organizations is the services or products that they produce. The output should always relate to the objectives of organizations; and organizations now are starting to develop objectives not only around profitability or high levels of service but also around factors such as a good working environment for staff and social responsibilities and contributions to the community. They are slowly becoming more aware of these issues, to the extent that these issues sometimes become objectives and are considered to be important output. If an organization doesn't treat people well it may have some short term gains, but it more likely has the potential of suffering long term losses. The reason for this is it is possible to push people harder and get more out of them in the short run but people become burned out, become antagonistic and may start sabotaging the system or actually leave the system.

The main feedback to an organization is from clients, the people who buy or use the product or service. Organizations also get some feedback from governments and regulating bodies such as business and professional associations. Organizations are often very active in soliciting feedback through market research. They build their feedback system and have people who are specialists in getting feedback for the organization.

Next, we must consider the boundary of the organization. The flexibility or the rigidity of organizational boundaries varies considerably. There are various ways to think about the organization boundaries. One aspect of boundaries is the physical boundary and its distance from other organizations. Organizations which are geographically separate often tend to be more autonomous. One example is a school. One of the reasons why a principal has so much power in a school is because it is geographically separate from the central office. The head of the organization isn't on the next floor up and this makes a big difference. The same is true with penitentiaries. The warden of the penitentiary has considerable power and part of the reason is geographical separation. However, boundaries are usually thought of more in terms of social and psychological aspects. There are some organizations which have very rigid boundaries. They would have very clear induction procedures for new members, very distinctive dress, strict behavior codes and a very formalized internal system.

In terms of assessing an organization one of the most important aspects is its environment. An organization must determine the environmental needs that the organization can satisfy. Traditionally, organizational change practice has neglected this area and looks only at the internal workings of the organization.[2] But it is impossible to consider the organization in isolation and many of the problems of organizations are not so much in terms of internal issues as much as the fit between the organization and its environment. For instance, an organization must determine who are its clients and what changes in clients can be anticipated so that the organization can continue to adapt and survive. Schools are currently undergoing this very issue in terms of the declining population of school-aged children. This change is one that should have been, but in many cases was not, anticipated. Another aspect of the environment is determining who are the suppliers. Who supplies the resources that are necessary to survive. These may include money, people, machines, and raw materials. In terms of the environment then, the two keys are the suppliers that provide the input and the clients that purchase the output.

Developmental stage

Looking at the next aspect of the model, which is the development stage of the system, it is very difficult to understand organizations developmentally. The way one can probably best do so is to look at an organization that began as a one person operation and gradually grew, over a period of time. In such cases one can see fairly clear developments. The major changes occur when that one person can't handle everything anymore and additional staff is brought in. Then the organization becomes more specialized, and more people are brought in to perform different functions. All the information is no longer in this one person's head. After the expansion takes place, there are often other changes in the products or services the organization provides. There may be changes in geography as the organization expands to different locations. And there is a danger of becoming overly rigid and bureaucratic with the growth. Some authors have written about the development cycles of organizations in terms of human development. The problem is that the stage of an organization has so much to do with leadership at this specific time, and it is hard to make those kinds of generalizations in terms of the developmental cycle. We don't know very much about that yet. One of the real paradoxes making it even more difficult is the fact that the average life expectancy of a person is nearly 70 years. If you were to look at the life expectancy of a business, it would probably be 2-3 years. Businesses that die usually do so within one year. Others are gone by 5. Such statistics about the life and death of organizations make it difficult to apply developmental concepts of people to the life span of organizations.

General factors

The fourth area of the model is consideration of the eight general factors. These include: objectives, structure, roles, communication, reward system, power, time, and space.

The first factor, objectives, is a critical one for an organization. Objectives are the basis of the whole planning process. It is very difficult to have meaningful strategies, tactics and long range plans without objectives. Many organizations don't do this type of planning and in times of a stable economy they may be able to get away with it. But when the economy isn't as good they can't afford this approach. Let me give you an example. Many accounting firms have grown at about 10 per cent a year over the past 5-6 years. The reality now is that economic growth is slowing down and this directly affects the growth of the accounting firm. Growth now requires more than keeping the front door open so that clients can keep flowing through. It requires good management that can find ways to do more with less, clear planning with outlined, or precast, objectives which are to be accomplished, and strategies for accomplishing these objectives.

There is a paradox in the literature around objectives. On the one hand, one of the most significant interventions in an organization is to help people set good objectives for themselves in terms of their own performance.[3] By good objectives I mean objectives that are attainable yet challenging, specific and measureable. They must be related to what the total organization wants to accomplish but also be personal and meaningful to the individual. There is considerable evidence supporting the value of this approach in motivating individuals. The paradox is that one of the interventions that often fails is setting up a Management by Objectives (MBO) system. What often happens in that situation is that an organization will develop a complex MBO system and the system becomes more important than the people it is designed to serve. The system becomes ritualized and there are absolute right and wrong ways to set and negotiate objectives. It is laid on in a fairly autocratic manner. So if you are going to work with an organization in setting objectives, try to keep it flexible. Don't be too concerned in the first year about an elaborate, formal system. The moral of the story is that if you want to bring about change you have got to do it in steps, and if you try to do everything at once you will probably fail.

The next aspect to consider, structure, is a critical one to a consultant. The basic point is that the structure of an organization (form) should be determined by the task the organization is trying to accomplish (function). The structure of an organization is also related to its environment. There is no right or wrong structure, only a right or wrong structure in a particular situation. For instance, there is a current trend to having 'flatter' organizations, where there are fewer levels of people and, therefore, less distance between the people at the top and bottom of the organization. This structure works best in constantly changing environments, where a few people cannot control all the information and where new procedures must be developed quickly. On the other hand, there are situations where the most effective organization is still the traditional hierarchial one. Those tend to be situations where the environment is fairly static as opposed to turbulent, where what was done 20 years ago will work just as well today and things are not changing very much, except perhaps in terms of the marketing of a product. An example of that would be a soft drink bottling company. They have an assembly line. They have a process. They have been making bottles using a similar process for years. People know how to operate the machines. There are changes now and again but the equipment is basically the same. The client needs don't fluctuate a great deal, at least relative to the chemical industry or the aerospace industry, where conditions may change quickly from day to day. A bottling company is, therefore, in a relatively static environment and can function effectively with a more hierarchial organization. So, there has to be a fit among the structure, the objectives and the environment in which the organization is operating.

The third area to consider is roles and responsibilities. One of the common problems in organizations is that people aren't clear about what they should be doing and about their responsibilities and accountabilities. One of the reasons for this is that most people work in fairly complex organizations where the lines of authority aren't as clear as they used to be. It is not at all uncommon in today's society for a given individual to have more than one boss in an organization. An example of this is working for a national organization and being responsible for sales in one region. There are two superiors. First of all, the individual is responsible to the person who is in charge of the Regional Office to whom reports are made on a daily basis. As well, the individual is responsible to the national head of sales for the effectiveness and efficiency of the sales effort. So sometimes there is a split in reporting relationships between a line relationship on a day to day basis and a staff relationship with more of a quality control relationship in terms of a specialty function of the organization.

In a hospital one often finds a matrix structure which has two lines of authority instead of the traditional one. One line of authority is what is known as a functional line of authority and involves the specialty departments in an organization. For example, there is a pediatrics department, a psychiatry department, a surgery department, and others. As well, hospitals are often organized around specific services. For instance, there is an intensive care unit, an outpatient department, and so on. So, if I am a psychologist in a hospital, I would probably report in a functional line to the head of psychology for the hospital. As well, I would report in a service line to the head of the outpatient clinic because that is where I work on a day to day basis. So, in point of fact, I have two bosses. One is the head of the department who assesses my day to day work and the other is the head of psychology who assesses the quality of my psychological work. So, it is becoming more and more common today in our larger and more complex organizations for people to have more than one reporting relationship. What this means is that it becomes even more critical to clarify roles and responsibilities since there is more chance for confusion and problems. It is amazing that many organizations that one would expect to be fairly sophisticated in this area have not really done a good job. When questioned, people often say that they really don't know who they are supposed to report to, or more commonly, what their specific responsibilities are. This leads to confusion, anxiety, wasted effort, and conflict.

In terms of communication it is necessary to consider an organization from two perspectives. The first is the formal communication system which includes both written (policy and procedures documents) and oral (regular group meetings) forms. One of the critical questions to ask is whether or not individuals have sufficient information to make the decisions that they are required to make. What one often finds (especially in larger organizations) is that there is a complex computerized information system, but that it sends managers information that is not relevant (all managers receive a huge document that is difficult to understand and sort through for appropriate information) and not timely (financial information with reference to budgets and expenditures often arrives one to three months after the month-end when it is most relevant).

The second aspect to understand communication in organizations is to determine the informal communication system in organizations. This involves understanding the informal relationships between people in organizations and determining who is the recipient of what kinds of information. I often find in organizations that the informal network is very important. For instance, I have been involved in a situation where the prisoners in a penitentiary knew about changes before the guards; another situation where the union knew about changes before middle management; and a third situation in which the secretaries knew about a change before their bosses. Keep your eyes and ears open.

The reward system in an organization is very important in generating the types of behavior that are required for the successful operation of the organization. The reward system can include many factors including pay, benefits, promotional opportunities, working conditions, opportunities for responsibility and autonomy, intrinsic value of the job, praise and support and interactions with a peer group. It is important to determine what the organization wants from its members; whether the organization understands the needs of the staff and rewards them appropriately; and, whether the system in fact rewards the type of behavior it says it wants. In terms of what the organization rewards, it is clear that different people are motivated by different factors. Some may place a higher value on pay than promotional opportunities, some may value them in the reverse order. The point is that organizations must recognize these differences in people and not treat all staff exactly the same.

The next dimension is power. Power is a reality of organizational life which many organization development consultants have tended to ignore. Many of these consultants have come out of human relations training backgrounds, which emphasize having people sit down and discuss their feelings. At times this is very functional but at other times can be very dysfunctional. Many solutions of this nature do not work because of the reality of power in organizations. Power rests at the top of the organization and is delegated down. In an effective organization power will be delegated down appropriately, that is, people who have the best information to make a decision should make it. The people who have the best information are usually the people who are closest to the situation. Many decisions that get passed up to a higher level in an organization create inefficiency, low morale and poor decision making. People at upper levels often don't have the information necessary to make the decision and shouldn't use their time, at their salary level, to make it. Furthermore, people at lower levels resent not having the opportunity to make decisions that do fall within their domain.

In terms of time, some problems that organizations experience result from insufficient consideration of the future. The corollary to that is that organizations often spend too much time dwelling on the past. One common and dysfunctional line one often hears in an organization is, "Well, why change, that is the way we have been doing it for years." At times this logic will work if the environment has not changed significantly. However, this is usually not the case, and organizations run the risk of going the way of the dinosaur. So, organizations need to have a good future perspective. They need to be able to anticipate future trends so that they can position themselves in advantageous ways. They also need a very good sense of what is going on presently. The present awareness is the basis on which they do the future planning. This awareness should encompass both the organization and its environment.

The use of space is important in terms of how effectively it is utilized and what it says about the values of an organization. Organizations are becoming more concerned with space in terms of attempts at office landscaping, lighting and intercom music systems.

Changes in space usage can have significant effects on an organization. An example is the use by schools of open area classrooms. This change in space had both positive and negative effects on staff and students. The use of open area design is a good example of the indiscriminate overuse of a reasonable idea. It is reasonable that open spaces support a more flexible program. Also, a physical openness may contribute to more interpersonal openness if there is some relationship between the physical environment and the psychology of people. But, what happened is that they took the idea and concluded that it was good for everyone. They forgot that some people need structure and order just as others need openness and flexibility. Furthermore, the assumption was made that staff and students would have no trouble adjusting to the new physical space. This is not true. When changes effect expectations with regard to peoples' behavior, the people often need help in adapting. So, this is a good example of change in space usage which had some potential for good but, because of not taking the people into account, it, at best, did not live up to its potential, and, at worst, has resulted in many failures.

Client-consultant relationship

The client-consultant relationship is diagrammed in Figure 8:3. The organization in the diagram is more simple than the actual organizations in which most consultants work. Due to the complexity, a critical consultant task is to determine 'who' is the client. The client could be the total organization, a branch or division of it, a specific work group within it, or even an individual within it.

There are two important factors to be considered in the client-consultant relationship. They are power and communication. In terms of power, it is critical that the consultant have a sufficient

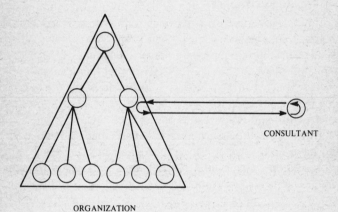

ORGANIZATION

FIGURE 8:3 Consultant relationship with organization

power base in which to operate. This usually means, as a minimum, having the support of the head of the particular organization with which the consultant is working and also the boss of that person. The failure to initially generate a sufficient power base is one of the major causes of failure in organizational interventions. A further point with regard to the power base is that it, initially, may be appropriate to involve other important stakeholders (unions) in the change process.

In terms of communication, it is important for the consultant to establish at the beginning who is going to receive what information. This is one of the reasons for determining who the client is. There are options for the sharing of information ranging from having all information totally public to reporting the information only to the president of the company. I have used the full range of options at different times, and I think it is important to individually assess each situation to determine how best to operate.

We will next consider the assessment of change potential, which involves motivation, skill, and power.

In terms of motivation, I have found that there are two critical factors. The obvious one is felt need or pain. A consultant is often called in when an organization clearly has problems. For instance, I have worked with accounting firms as the economy took a downturn and with correctional centers after riots or staff walk-outs.

The other factor that seems to be related to motivation is the image held by the organization of the type of organization that it wants to be. For instance, some organizations function well, but have such a high commitment to excellence or certain types of values that they enhance their operation even though there is no strong deficiency.

In terms of skill, I often find that organizations are deficient in management skills. More often than not this results from the promotion of an individual from a non-management position without the appropriate training. There are many examples. Doctors become hospital administrators; teachers become principals; and engineers and sales staff become managers. This pattern often creates a great deal of anxiety and potential problems for both the individual and the organization.

In terms of power, it is critical to determine that the areas with which you are concerned have, in fact, the necessary power to execute the changes they desire. If not it will be necessary first to develop an appropriate power base.

Since the assessment at the organizational level is more complex and often more distinct than the assessments at the levels we have considered up to this point, I would like to discuss the process before moving on to look at the intervention.

In terms of assessing an organization one of the key questions is how to collect the information. I generally prefer to interview a random sample of people in the organization including all key people and people from all levels of the organization. Often the comments from people at the top of the organization are very different from the comments of people at the bottom of the organization. One of the jobs of a consultant is to put together discrepant bits of information. Another thing you would probably want to do is to look at certain organizational files or documents that could be helpful in terms of assessing an organization. The third thing that you sometimes would do, and I normally don't do, unless working with a very large organization, is to distribute a questionnaire. The advantage of questionnaires is that they give you more specific data. The disadvantage is that they are not quite as flexible as the interview process from which one picks up many nuances. You can get the subtleties and probe a little deeper and get some new information.

The reaction I get when I go into an organization varies considerably in each situation. I think many people, when I come in to assess and particularly to work with an organization, feel skeptical. "We have been doing it this way for a while. Who the hell do you think you are to help us do anything better?" Sometimes though there is hope. We have talked about hope in terms of individual change earlier, and often, especially if people are in a fairly desperate negative situation, a consultant generates hope. I was involved in a situation with a jail where the staff was in a tremendous conflict with the superintendent. It led to sit downs, threatened walkouts, and many other problems. I was asked to do some initial assessment and eventually work with them. In that particular case my becoming involved in the situation was a hopeful sign for the staff. This was not because of who I was but because the organization had considered the problem important enough to have someone outside come into the organization.

Another way responses vary is in the degree to which people try to 'snow you' during the assessment. Sometimes there are overt attempts to present incorrect information. Sometimes it is not even intentional. I have had people tell me that everything was just fine and I am sure that they believed it even if it didn't appear that way to most others. Other times people try to 'snow you' because they are afraid that they have something to lose. Sometimes consultants are seen as a threat.

Another important point is that every time you conduct an assessment, and as a result of that take on a project, your professional reputation is on the line. Part of your responsibility as a professional is to say no when no is appropriate. As an example, a national retail organization asked me to give them a proposal on doing management training with their staff. I said I would only give them a proposal if I could talk to a random sample of people initially to find out more about what was happening in the organization. I talked with these people, thought about it, made some decisions, wrote a brief report and met with the president and the executive group. I opened my presentation by saying, "My presentation to you will essentially outline the reasons why you shouldn't conduct management training at this time." They were quite shocked, especially since they already had two proposals from consultants outlining what wonderful management training jobs they would do. I said that after looking at their organization it was my professional judgment that the organization didn't have objectives, didn't have an optimum organization structure, and lacked clarity about roles and responsibilities. If I did management training and was successful in turning on the managers and helping them to value effective management practices, I predicted that many of them would have left within six months, frustrated over the management practices and their inability to change them. What I recommended they do was to develop a management system that could support a training program. Needless to say, they were quite shocked and the president was, at times, quite defensive about some of the points. It was threatening in that situation for anyone to agree with the outsider, the consultant, so the vice presidents were reluctant to say anything. Finally, one of them, who has been with the company for years and years and was a crusty old guy, said, "You know, I want to tell you something. I have been with this company for 35 years and everything that you have said is true." That was the clincher, and what they did as a result was to spend a year developing a planning system, clarifying their objectives and doing some work on their structure. They are now getting around to the point where it might be appropriate to do some management training.

One of the points in terms of doing an assessment, then, is that it is just as important to say no as it is to say yes. If you are always going to say yes, and if you are always going to make the same intervention, there is no point in doing assessments. The implication of an assessment is that you both make a decision whether or not to do something and if you decide to proceed then consider the intervention specifics.

Usually I will set up two-part contract with an organization. One of the biggest downfalls of many management consultants is that they submit reports and run. I have been in too many organizations where expensive management consultant reports are sitting on shelves gathering dust. What has to happen is that first you need to be aware of what the problem is and what to do about it, and, second, and this is just as important, you have to help the organization to do it. The doing is usually harder than the knowing what to do. Management consultants often only tell people what to do, and since plans never work out perfectly there are always modifications that need to be made. So what I do first of all is assess the situation. At the end of that time I make recommendations as to what should be done. The recommendations will essentially be based on the results of interviews and observations. People in the organization often know quite well what has to be done. My job is pull that out and put it together. I make it clear at the outset that I am not willing to prepare recommendations unless there is an understanding that an organization has 'a commitment to action.' This doesn't mean that they have to hire me; it doesn't mean that they have to hire any outside person; it doesn't even mean they have to accept all the recommendations. But, if they are just interested in gathering some information and thinking about it, then I am not interested in working with them. So essentially, what I am saying is that if I am going to do a study for an organization, I want their commitment to action. This is one of my conditions because I am not interested in doing an assessment that is going to gather dust. At the end of the first stage, when the assessment is done and the recommendations are in, then we sit down and we talk about the future. Often what I do in recommendations is separate the activities that the organization should do itself and the activities for which they should have a consultant. This helps to clarify resource requirements and leads to effective change processes.

Intervention

The intervention into an organization follows directly from and is based upon the assessment. Before discussing some of the potential interventions, it would be useful to discuss some of the guidelines which I find important in developing the intervention process. Five points will be considered.

The first point is that the consultant should limit recommendations to only the most critical issues; the failure to do so can overwhelm an organization. I often find in assessing an organization that it would be possible to make one hundred recommendations. I consciously work on narrowing my list to between 10 and 20 of the most critical points. My experience has been that if these are in fact the most critical issues, and if the organization develops some momentum in dealing with these issues, that many of the more minor issues will be dealt with in the process as a result of the increased skill that the organization develops in sensing and rectifying problem situations.

The second point is that the recommendations should be specific as to what needs to be done, who is responsible for doing it, and by when will it be completed. Some of the recommendations may be handled by the consultant (those requiring special external expertise such as management development) and some may be handled directly by the organization members (those which the organization members have sufficient expertise to implement).

The third point is that the intervention must be of sufficient duration to affect the required changes. Many consultants make the mistake of trying to bring about an organization change with an intervention of very short duration (a week-end or week-long workshop). Much of the literature on organization change suggests that successful interventions require three to five years. While this time frame may be necessary for large organizations, my experience has been that it is possible to bring about a significant change in smaller organizations (less than five hundred employees) in twelve to eighteen months.

The fourth point is that it is critical to begin the intervention at the top and work down through the organization. There are several reasons for this. In the first place, many of the critical organizational decisions must be made at the top (overall organization planning, policy, procedures, structure); since these factors affect the rest of the organization it is important to start at the top. As well, in order for the intervention to be successful throughout the organization there must be an active commitment from the senior management group. The best way to demonstrate this is to have the senior management group involved in the process from the beginning.

The fifth and final point is that I usually find it helpful to establish an internal-external consulting team. This format takes advantage of both the external person's expertise and credibility and the internal person's knowledge and experience with the organization. At times the external person can assist in the skill development of the internal person, and thereby increase the probability that the necessary facilitating skills will remain in the organization subsequent to the departure of the external consultant.

We will next briefly consider the intervention implications from the systems analysis. Interventions may be related to input (increasing marketing activities to increase number of sales), throughput (operations research to increase efficiency of operation), output (better quality control procedures), feedback (more effective market research), boundary (increasing identification with organization), and environment (more effective assessment of changes and trade trends in the environment). Naturally, one consultant would not be able to assist in all of these areas. However, it is often important to facilitate interventions by either members of the organization or other external consultants to remedy problems in these areas which are vital to an organization's functioning.

Next, we will discuss the potential interventions related to the eight general factors in the assessment model. These include clarifying objectives, restructuring the organization, clarifying roles and responsibilities, communication process intervention, modifying the reward system, changing power distribution, and time and space alterations.

In terms of clarifying objectives, two levels are important to consider. The first is the organizational level, in terms of the objectives for the organization as a whole and for the divisions or departments of the organization. The second is setting objectives at the individual level, working with individuals to set objectives against which they will be able to assess their performance. Setting objectives is one of the most effective interventions one can make in an organization to increase effectiveness.

A second possible intervention involves restructuring the organization. There are two main principles that can guide a restructuring process. The first is that the groups or departments in an organization must logically fit together. For instance, administrative functions would tend to be clustered together in an organization, and would tend not to be grouped with production functions. The second point is that supervisors and managers should have an appropriate number of subordinates reporting to them (span of control). While there are no absolute numbers that are appropriate in all situations, an average range would be 4 to 8 subordinates.

The third possible intervention involves clarifying people's roles and responsibilities. While one might assume that this is such a straightforward issue that most organizations would have successfully dealt with it, my experience has been that people in organizations often are not clear about either what their functions are, or more importantly, how much authority they have to carry out the functions. The process of clarifying roles and responsibilities involves a series of negotiations between superiors and subordinates at various levels of the organization.

The fourth possible intervention involves improving the communication system. The two major aspects of this include improving small group meeting functioning (discussed in Chapter Six) and information flow. The latter usually involves developing information systems so that organizational members receive information as required that is both timely and relevant.

The fifth possible area of intervention involves modifying the reward system. This may involve looking at the compensation and benefits system or modifying the performance appraisal system. Many organizations do not provide adequate assessment and feedback for staff, and do not base rewards on performance. Therefore, modification of the performance appraisal system can result in a significant improvement in the functioning of an organization.

The sixth possible area of intervention relates to the power function. One aspect of power in an organization is decision-making authority. The main rule to remember is that decisions should be made as close to the source of best information as possible. Often decisions get bounced up too high in the organization, and senior staff make inconsequential day-to-day operational decisions and neglect more wide-reaching planning and control issues. This results in wasted effort and neglect of important functions. The use of role and responsibility clarification can often assist in the redistribution of decision making authority.

The last two possible areas of intervention relate to the time and space dimensions. In terms of time, it is often appropriate to assist an organization to develop a more effective future orientation; this naturally relates to the planning process. In terms of space, there may be opportunities to modify the space utilization and to promote more flexibility and efficiency in its usage.

In concluding this section, one final point should be noted. From the assessment of change potential, I often discover that there is a deficiency in supervisory and management skill in an organization. This is a critical area and can often mean the difference between success and failure in a project. The intervention may be to actually conduct management training sessions, or to have key people sent to appropriate training experiences. Training conducted on site as part of an intervention process provides a unique opportunity to teach supervisory and management skills on the basis of real organizational situations rather than simulations, and thereby integrate interventions at both the individual and organizational levels.

NOTES

1. Attempts to enlarge and enrich jobs and develop work teams tend to fall under the rubric of quality of working life. A good review of the area can be found in a two-volume series *The Quality of Working Life* by L.E. Davis and A.E. Cherns, eds. (New York: The Free Press, 1975).
2. Currently the relationships between organizations and their environments is a popular academic area. One of the seminal thinkers in the area has been J.D. Thompson *Organizations in Action* (New York: McGraw Hill, 1967).
3. A recent review of the organizational behavior literature including the area of goal setting is found in "Organizational Behavior" by T.R. Mitchell in the *Annual Review Psychology* (Palo Alto: Annual Reviews, Inc. 1979, 30, 243-82).

150

QUESTIONS

1. Apply the consultants' human systems assessment model (Figure 8:1) to an organization with which you are familiar. What are the major problem areas of the organization?
2. If there are gaps in the assessment model modify it to better suit your purposes.
3. Assess your skills in each of the potential change areas mentioned. Do you have a strategy and technology for each of the areas?
4. In working with an organization are there change areas that you consider important? Describe your strategies and technologies in these areas.

ANNOTATED BIBLIOGRAPHY

Addison-Wesley Series on Organization Development
    Originally six books, then nine, and now further ones are being added, all of which provide excellent background and reference sources. One of the best introductory books in the series is *Organization Development: Strategies and Models* (1969) by R. Beckhard.
Adams, J.D., ed. *Theory and Method in Organization Development.* Arlington, Va.: NTL Institute, 1974.
    A good book of readings on organization development.
Administrative Science Quarterly
    One of the best administrative journals, it has a research orientation and tends to be quite academic. Contains many seminal articles.
Burke, W.W. *Contemporary Organization Development: conceptual orientations and interventions.* Arlington, Va.: NTL Institute, 1972.
    The first book of readings in the area; many of the articles have considerable relevance.
Burke, W.W. & Hornstein, H.A. *The Social Technology of Organizational Development.* Fairfax, Va.: NTL Institute, 1972.
    Another book of readings; they're all useful, take your pick.
Galbraith, J.R. *Organization Design.* Reading, Mass.: Addison-Wesley, 1977.
    This would have to rate as one of the best books in the field. Provides a comprehensive view of organizations. Must reading!
Harvard Business Review
    A practical journal that presents many outstanding articles on various aspects of management and organization behavior and change.
Huse, E.F. *Organization Development and Change.* St. Paul: West Publishing Co. 1975.
    Probably the most comprehensive test book on organization development available.
Katz, D. & Kahn, R.L. *The Social Psychology of Organizations.* New York: Wiley, 1966.
    A classic textbook on understanding the functioning of organizations. Provides some heavy reading but worth the effort.
Passmore, W.A. & Sherwood, J.J. *Sociotechnical Systems: A Sourcebook.* La Jolla, Ca.: University Associates, 1978.
    A welcome addition to the field, provides a look at the relationship between social and technical systems; too much of the previous emphasis has been on the social system in isolation from the technical.

CHAPTER NINE

Interorganization change

The dynamics of assessing and intervening at the interorganization level are quite similar to those at the intergroup level. The major difference is in terms of the increased complexity of dealing with organizations. Interorganization relationships include two social service agencies providing services in the same community; an organization and a client organization; an organization and a supplier organization; two government organizations; and even two competing organizations.

We will consider both the assessment and intervention aspects of dealing with the interorganization relationships.

Assessment

In Figure 9:1 we see the consultants' human systems assessment model. This model involves specifying the system level, completing a systems analysis, determining the developmental stage, considering several general factors and looking at the client-consultant relationship.

Before considering these factors let us look at a diagrammatic representation of the interorganization relationship.[1] This is shown in Figure 9:2. The major difference between this model and the one considered in Figure 7:2 for the intergroup level is that at the interorganization level there are several organizational levels to consider while in a group there are seldom more than two levels. Therefore, there are many more combinations and permutations for contact between organizations than between groups. This makes the assessment a more difficult process and also places potential limitations on intervention processes.

1) Systems level: interorganization

2) Systems analysis:
   a) Input
   b) Throughput
   c) Output
   d) Feedback
   e) Boundary
   f) Environment

3) Developmental stage

4) General factors:
   a) Objectives
   b) Structure
   c) Roles
   d) Communication
   e) Reward system
   f) Power
   g) Time
   h) Space

5) Client-Consultant relationship

FIGURE 9:1 Consultants' human systems assessment model: interorganization level

155

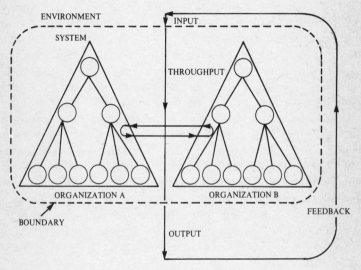

FIGURE 9:2 Interorganization human system

Let us now consider the five factors of the model and the assessment of change potential.

Systems level

The systems level is the interorganization level.

Systems analysis

The systems analysis involves looking at input, throughput, output, feedback, boundary, and environment.

The input to the interorganization relationship includes community needs, values, political pressures, money, and staff. The throughput of the interorganization system includes all interaction that takes place between the organizations. This may be difficult to track due to the number of possible levels at which the contact occurs. The output of the system would be decisions, planning and actions which, hopefully, lead to mutual benefit for both systems. The feedback comes from clients, sponsors, and the general public. However, often interorganizational activities take place in a more private than public forum, and, therefore, the feedback is often delayed and loses some of its impact. The boundary of an interorganization system tends to be quite loose. The environment of the interorganizational system contains some common factors and some unique to only one of the organizations. Often parts of the environment are nebulous, and it is sometimes difficult to determine which are the critical factors in the environment.

Developmental stage

As with the intergroup situation the developmental stages have not been clearly described. It is probably, therefore, most useful to consider the history of the relationship and any previous attempts at problem solving.

General factors

There are eight general factors to consider. These include objectives, structure, roles, communication, reward system, power, time, and space.

There are several problems in looking at objectives in the interorganization level. In the first place, the objectives usually are not explicitly stated by organizations. While one would think that this would be one of the most basic things that organizations would do, such is not the case. It may be necessary to go back to the individual organizations first to determine what their objectives are. The second potential problem is that there is often a difference between the stated objectives and the real objectives. For instance, two mental health organizations may have as their prime objective to increase the level of mental health care in the community. And you as a consultant breathe a sigh of relief and think about how easy collaboration between these two organizations will be. What you don't realize is that the real objectives in each organization are to maintain current staffing levels; maintain complete control in the community of certain delivery systems; and to demonstrate a need for more money than the other agencies. So, don't be fooled by initial positive sounding objectives.

There is both a structural relationship between the organizations and a structure within each organization. Occasionally a formal structure (interorganizational coordinating council) is set up between the organizations to deal with the interorganizational relations. One of the implications of the complex structure of organizations is that many points of contact are possible between them and it is necessary to determine if perceptions are similar at various levels. For instance, it is possible that the workers at the lower levels of the organization have regular sharing of information and get along well, while the directors of the organizations are very territorial and competitive and don't get along as well.

In terms of roles, it is important to determine what are the roles of the two organizations. This is often difficult to determine because different people have different views. For instance, a community clinic may be seen as having roles of providing care to the community, training professionals and monitoring the quality of services of other organizations. This multiple role may be viewed differently by staff, patients, other organizations and community leaders. Furthermore, if the roles of organizations are not clearly defined (as is often the case) and there are two organizations in the same community with fairly similar roles, you can be almost certain of a conflict situation. So we have to be concerned not only with what the role is (and trying to define that) but also determining the majority perception of the role.

One of the major problems is that communication is poor. There is often mistrust (based more often on fantasy than on reality), which reduces both the frequency (it is surprising how little communication takes place between organizations in a similar area) and quality (messages are usually guarded and sometimes not correct) of communication between organizations.

In terms of the reward system, it is important to determine how an organization receives its revenues. In the private sector the clients, and therefore client service, becomes a foremost concern. In the public sector being able to maintain (and hopefully increase) government funding is a prime consideration. This information can often provide clues as to causes of conflict and their potential solution.

The dimension of power is extremely important at the interorganization level, as it was at the intergroup level. The relative power of the two organizations is critical in determining any change process outcome. A consultant must determine the sources of power of the two organizations and, in particular, any needs that are met by the partner organization.

Finally, it is useful to consider the nature of time spent together by the organizations and also the space where this meeting occurs. It may also be useful to determine which organization initiates the contacts.

Client-consultant relationship

The client-consultant relationship is diagrammed in Figure 9:3. It shows that the two organizations have relationships with each other, and the consultant has a relationship with each of the organizations. As with the intergroup level, this diagram is less complicated than the actual situation since each organization contains multiple levels, significantly increasing the number of relationship contacts which may affect the overall interorganization relationship.

Before moving on to the intervention section let us consider the change potential in terms of motivation, skill, and power. As with formal groups often one organization will have more motivation than the other; both organizations usually have sufficient skill; and there is often a power imbalance in that the organization resisting has sufficient power to do so. Often the first thing the consultant needs to do is attempt to modify the power relationship.

Intervention

Many of the points made at the intergroup level also apply to the interorganization intervention. The assessment is critical and must

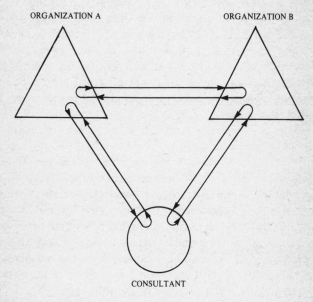

FIGURE 9:3 Consultant relationship with interorganization system

be of a high quality. Useful strategies include tightening up the boundary; developing more commonality of objectives; maintaining internal strength; improving communication; and, making the reward system conducive to change.

Instead of repeating the details of these points I will cite two examples from my practice and then make some final comments.

The first example demonstrates the importance of determining whether you will be dealing with the total group or just part of it. This decision in itself can present a trap. For example, I was once called upon to work with two social service agencies. They called me in because it was necessary for them to cooperate but they weren't doing so. As a result their services had deteriorated. So both agencies had some vested interest in better performance. The interesting thing about this situation is that the two directors of the agencies decided that their staffs should get together and meet, but they felt there was no need for either director to meet. So, right away the red flag was raised and I wondered what was going on. Why didn't they want to get together? In point of fact, when we got into exploring it, many of the problems were between the directors. And, if they weren't at least to attend the session and, better still, have a prior meeting to work out some of their own differences, there was no point in the groups getting together. It would have been a deflection of the real problem. I would have been treating the symptom not the problem. The other thing that I would have been doing by having that kind of meeting, is allowing them to define the problem as a staff problem and not a leadership problem. So professional credibility would have been added to their misdiagnosis. So the first choice then is whether or not you work with the two people who are the heads of the agencies or the total agencies, and if you work with the total agencies, the heads normally have to be included in the process.

When you have made this decision and get the two groups together, you often want to help people change perceptions. Often perceptions have been inaccurate and built up over many, many years. A simple exercise for doing this is to have the two groups go off on their own and write out a list showing how they see themselves, how they see the other group, and how they think the other group sees them. Then have them get together and share the data. It is a very informative exercise. Usually what you will find happening is that each group will see themselves as good guys, see the other group as bad guys, and think that the other group sees them as bad guys. It inevitably works out that way, and what usually happens is that they are quite surprised to see the stereotyping.

A second situation in which I was involved was a conflict between two organizations. The conflict had been going on for about eighteen months and they asked me to go away to a retreat with these people. There were fifteen of them and they had done some initial work. One of the things I did was get a little history on what had already happened. My judgment was that their relationship probably had been worse about six months before and was gradually getting better. It still had a long way to go but it was on an upward swing. Because it was on an upward swing I didn't want to go through the changing perceptions exercise. The exercise is usually useful to go through when you are starting at zero. The thing that the exercise would have done is to have brought them back closer to zero and then I would have had to work up again. I didn't want to do that. One rule I had was that for the first general session they could not have any planned presentations. I didn't want them coming in with prepared cases because that would have further separated them to start. So there was no opportunity to make group presentations initially. The strategy that I decided on in order to assist them was first of all to have a common session with everyone, where they would define their problems. Then I got them to work in task forces where they worked on specific problems. What were the high priority problems that were getting in the way of the two groups working together effectively? What could they do about this? Then I had them come back to the total group, make the presentations and then decide on the best change strategies.

In setting up the two task forces, the rule was that there had to be an equal number from each group on each task force. These two task forces, over a period of a couple of days, developed a very competitive relationship. The issue became who was going to make the best presentation. It was a fascinating experience because all of the polarities and stereotyping between the two initial groups disappeared. There was more of a camaraderie. They were working together, they were learning that this person from the other group wasn't such a rotten person after all. They were able to come up with some very good plans and there was some ongoing structure built into them.

I am not saying this is a case that ended up perfectly, because I understand that they still have some conflicts. However, it is an example of a change strategy in which two groups working on some common issues together produced some positive effect. This is an important strategy to use.

One of the outcomes that we have talked about in this type of a situation is the need for an agreement that was mutual and beneficial to both sides. There is a further element to this. The further element is that not only must any agreement be beneficial to both sides, it must be 'perceived' as being beneficial to both sides. It is important that neither side lose face as a result of the negotiation. You find that seasoned negotiators often work very hard to save face for each other. They fight and the fights are real. But these negotiators also know that the other person's reputation is on the line and there is some advantage to being helpful at certain points. The worst thing in the world anyone can do is to humiliate an opponent, because chances are that they will come back and get you the next time around.

A couple of other points are important. People in a situation of this type need to recognize the legitimacy of the other person's needs, requests and demands. There is a tendency initially to think that everything that you want is okay, and everything the other person wants is an aberration. For you to help recognize the legitimacy of the other side is important. One of the techniques or tactics that you can sometimes use in changing the perceptions is doing a role-reversal exercise. This involves having the two parties role-play each other to understand what it would be like in the other person's position. Sometimes this can help to change perceptions and increase mutual understanding.

The final point in this process is the same as at the interpersonal level. It is important to develop a contract that is clear. In more formal situations you would want the contract to be written.

NOTES

1. A recent review "Community structure as interorganization linkages" by E.O. Lauman, J. Galaskiewicz and P.V. Marsden in the *Annual Review of Sociology* (1978, 4, 455-84) looks at the types of linkages between organizations.

164

QUESTIONS

1. Apply the consultants' human systems assessment model (Figure 9:1) to an interorganizational situation with which you are familiar.
2. On the basis of this modify the model to better suit your own situation. Describe your adapted model.
3. Apply elements of the intervention discussion to a situation in which you are involved. Which would have the greatest impact. Why?

ANNOTATED BIBLIOGRAPHY

Negandhi, A. *Interorganization Theory.* Kent, Ohio: Kent State University Press, 1975.
While this book deals with a fairly abstract level it is one of the few dealing exclusively with the interorganization area.

CHAPTER TEN

Community change

The final systems level we will consider is the community. We will consider the community from both the assessment and intervention points of view.

Assessment

In Figure 10:1 we have the consultants' human systems assessment model for the community level. The model includes the systems level, a systems analysis, the developmental stage, eight general factors, and the client-consultant relationship.

Before considering these factors let us look at the diagrammatic representation of the community found in Figure 10:2. We have chosen a very simple example of a community, one that contains two families and two organizations. Communities come in many different forms. Examples of communities include towns, neighborhoods, Indian reservations and condominium developments. A community is generally considered to be a distinct geographic area that is small enough for the residents to have some direct contact. As can be concluded from this, a community is a complex social system, incorporating many of the features of the individuals, families and organizations of which it is composed.

Let us now consider the five-part human system assessment model and also the assessment of change potential.

Systems level

The systems level under consideration is the community.

168

1) Systems level: community

2) Systems analysis:

   a) Input
   b) Throughput
   c) Output
   d) Feedback
   e) Boundary
   f) Environment

3) Developmental stage

4) General factors:

   a) Objectives
   b) Structure
   c) Roles
   d) Communication
   e) Reward system
   f) Power
   g) Time
   h) Space

5) Client-consultant relationship

   FIGURE 10:1 Consultants' human systems assessment model: organization level

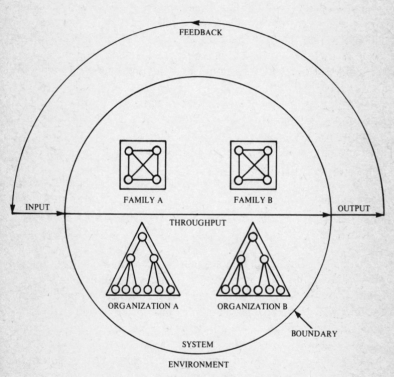

FIGURE 10:2 Community human system

Systems analysis

The systems analysis consists of looking at the input, throughput, output, feedback, boundary, and environment of the community.

The input into a community includes individuals, families, businesses, government agencies, money, and social, economic and political values and factors.

The throughput of a community includes its interactions and operations. There may be both formal (elected officials) and informal (network of friends) interactions in the community. The importance of values, and the great diversity of value positions, is much more clear at the community level than at any other. For example, a frequent area of conflict in a community involves personal and business values. (Should the vacant land be used for a park or for an office complex?) The decision around questions like this rests not only on values but also on power. What are the power blocks that support these different values? Most decisions of this nature are not, and cannot be, made simply on the basis of objective facts. This is political decision making based on values and power.

The output of the community includes the products or services coming from the community members. In order for a community to survive it is often important that some services or products be exported in order to bring money and other goods and services into the community. This is because the community cannot be totally self-sufficient but must interact with its environment in order to survive. Output of the community includes its cultural and recreational output. Output also includes the individuals or families who leave as well as the businesses that fail or relocate. When businesses conclude that conditions are unfavorable (taxes are too high or labor is not reliable), they may decide to leave. An example of this is the exodus in the United States from the northeastern to the southern states. This is a tremendous threat to communities in the north west, particularly for smaller communities that are dependent on one or two industries.

One of the major sources of feedback comes from economics. How is the community doing economically? Is it fully utilizing resources? What businesses can it attract? A second area of feedback for a community is demographic data. Is the population increasing or decreasing? A third area of feedback is in terms of the quality of life and includes considerations such as athletic and cultural activities, crime and pollution.

The boundary of a community is usually not very clear. Individuals, families and organizations move back and forth across the boundary on a regular basis. Membership in a community can often be obtained fairly easily. The time the boundary seems to tighten most is if the community perceives an external threat (a major organization closes down and the community leaders start to organize).

The environment of a community includes the larger political systems (states or provinces) and the particular social and cultural norms of the region or country. The environment of a community also includes large corporations that have some interest in the community. For instance, a large manufacturing company may have a plant in the community. While the plant itself is part of the community, the head office is part of the environment. It is also a very important part of the environment of the community since it has the power to pull the plant out of the community.

Developmental stage

The next aspect of assessment concerns the developmental stage. Communities are similar to organizations in that their developmental stages are not usually clear. There is a tendency for communities to survive for longer periods of time than organizations. You can often trace communities back to the origins of a given area. The basis for their survival is having resources that will provide them with a continuous viability. That is the key. They require some kind of resource, strength or competitive edge in order to survive. Often the choices are good and have long-term benefits for communities. Sometimes what was once an advantage will, later turn out to be a liability. It seems more likely that rather than going through a developmental sequence, communities go through a series of up-and-down cycles, where the outcome of one has a direct effect on future patterns.

General factors

There are eight general factors to consider. These include objectives, structure, roles, communication, reward system, power, time, and space. In introducing these factors it should be pointed out that a community is a diverse set of entities. Very seldom do we find clear power channels, clear objectives or clear structure. One can go into an organization and understand its major functions fairly quickly. There are organization charts, job descriptions, and the formal system that can be understood fairly quickly, although the informal system will take somewhat longer to comprehend. But the community is very difficult to understand because there are so many different aspects of the power system and the decision-making system.

It is difficult to determine the community objectives; as such they usually don't exist. Communities have very diverse values and therefore have very diverse objectives. There is not a single set of objectives that one could list for a community. Organizations should have sets of objectives. But a community must go through a political process in order to sort out values and set objectives and make decisions.

The structure of a community is often not very easy to determine, initially. There are many interrelationships and one of the real challenges is being able to draw the network between these various groupings and understand the communication system and the power system. Often the only aspect of the structure that is clear in a large community, initially, is the formal political structure. However, this is only part of the picture.

The roles in the community will vary tremendously. There are both formal and informal roles. The formal roles include roles in organizations and the political structure. Informal roles relate to who people know or who people influence.

A similar diffuse pattern exists with formal and informal lines of communication. It is necessary to try to figure out the network of the community. One simple way would be to take a random sample of people in the community and ask them who are groups of friends, and who has influence in the community. Downplay the number of nominations for official people since everyone is going to mention the mayor. People who are closer to the power network often provide the best source of information.

The next issue is the reward system of a community. It is necessary to understand what the reward system is within the community itself. This varies tremendously from community to community. For instance, in some communities illegal behavior is highly rewarded. Some communities have norms that smoking grass is acceptable. Other communities have norms around the types of athletic activities that are rewarded. If people want to be athletic stars and be noticed, they would be better off playing football than participating in swimming activities. There are varied reward systems tied into athletics as well. This varies considerably from community to community.

One of the key variables in understanding the functioning of a community is in terms of power. Power is a critical factor in pre-determining what decisions will be made and what actions will be taken in a community. This becomes a difficult variable to understand. There may or may not be an official power structure in a community. Examples of power structure would be the mayor and the council of a city, the chief and elders of an Indian tribe, and the president and board of directors of a condominium. Assuming such a formal power structure exists, this would be the first part of the analysis. The second part of the analysis would be to determine the informal power structure. Who really has the power or is the power behind the scene? For instance, in considering municipal politics, who were the most significant backers of the mayor and the council? Where are political favors owed? Remember, the primary objective of most politicians is to get re-elected. When one realizes this, political behavior seems more understandable. The formal system, if one exists, may simply be the tip of the iceberg in terms of really understanding community power.

In terms of time and space we find a great deal of variance depending on the community situation. In terms of time, usually people in a community will spend limited amounts of it with each other, and these times will usually be in relation to specific activities. The activities will be related to individual needs within the community. In terms of space, there is both public and private space. However, people may not share the space at the same time. One of the issues that is becoming more important for communities is the question of space utilization and space sharing. At one point in time, we thought if we wanted more of a certain type of space we could just build another building. Now, due mainly to economic factors, we say we can't afford this and we should make better use of our current available space. Therefore, we need better planning and greater cooperation.

Client-consultant relationship

In Figure 10:3 we have a diagrammatic representation of the relationship between a consultant and a community. We have again used, in our example, a fairly simple community consisting of two

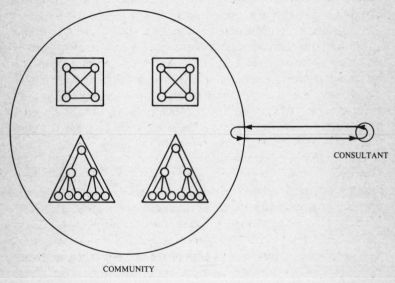

COMMUNITY

FIGURE 10:3 Consultant relationship with community

families and two organizations. In most cases the consultant will work with more complex systems.

Naturally, the consultant may have contact with many different parts of the community. As in consulting with organizations, it is important to determine who, actually, is the client. It could be the total community or it could be any one of the systems or relationships between systems in the community.

However, at the community level we run into a complication that has not surfaced to the same degree in the analysis of the previous six systems levels. That is the question of a sponsor. The sponsor is the entity (usually a government or private agency) that pays the consultant to work with the community. While the community may pay directly for the consultants' services, usually there is a sponsor. This tends not to happen at the organization level, where the client and sponsor tend to be one and the same (the organization). The reason that this is a complication is that there may be some situations in which the best interest of the sponsor and the client do not coincide. For instance, if the sponsoring agency is in fact not providing adequate services, and the client (community) wants to expose the situation, the consultant is in an interesting bind. To act as an advocate for the client may be in the client's best interests, but may not be in the best interest of the sponsor (they may lose part of their jurisdiction or mandate) or that of the consultant (the consultant may lose a client or a sponsor).

Before moving on to the intervention let us consider the assessment of change potential in terms of motivation, skills, and power. While there is certainly no set pattern, one often finds considerable motivation, yet a lack of skill and power.

In terms of motivation, it is important to determine on which issues there is sufficient felt need for the community to respond. It is likely that most communities are apathetic about many of the issues. However, there are usually some issues that have a high degree of need around which a community can be mobilized. It is important to assess whether or not the community members have the basic skills required to function in a change process. These include skills in communication, decision making, problem solving, running small group meetings and being able to develop appropriate strategic plans.

In terms of power, it is important to determine whether the community has sufficient power to make the desired changes. Often there are certain salient issues for which a necessary power is present, and others for which it is not. In such a circumstance it is usually advisable to start with the issues that have the appropriate power base.

Intervention

In terms of the implementation process, I would like to make a few comments about community development and community change. There are three separate approaches to community change and they are all based on different assumptions.[1] One approach to community change is community development. In community development, you help to mobilize the people. You develop a community resource and get the people together. You develop their leadership skills and you help them choose appropriate strategies. But, they must do things themselves; you must not do things for them. It is the community change version of client-centered therapy. The client knows best and your job is to facilitate and to help. There is a second approach to community change called social planning. In the social planning approach the assumption is that there is a great technical body of knowledge that is necessary to effect constructive change. You need to be an expert in order to use it, however. Therefore, as a community consultant in this role you do an analysis, get all the data, figure it out, arrive at a decision and then make a recommendation to the community (or sponsor) as to what they should do. This is an expert mode as opposed to the previous facilitative mode. This expert is not unlike the consultant who goes in to an organization, does an operations research study and says that the client should move the assembly line three feet to the left because it will be more efficient. The third area is particularly interesting since professionally trained 'helpers' tend to ignore it because they feel very uncomfortable with it. It is the social action change strategy which involves an advocacy role. A good example of this is the work of Saul Alinsky. The assumption that you make is that you are in a competitive situation and working with a group that doesn't have many resources. However, if you can mobilize their resources in some way you can help them beat the opposition. It is seen as a fight in which you need to develop the best strategy. In doing this it is necessary to be able to accurately assess both your own and the opposition's strengths and weaknesses. The next step, if possible, would be to attack your opponent's weakness with your strength.

A successful community consultant will not be locked into one role. The key is to be flexible and adapt one's behavior to the needs of the situation.

One of the critical first tasks for a consultant is to gain entry into the community. This often requires having some awareness of its formal and informal leadership and power systems. For instance, I was working with an Amerindian community. They had a formal structure with a chief who was in charge of that particular tribe. But the real power network centered around a young man who was the chief's heir apparent and actually ran things. He didn't have a formal title, but in terms of getting things done he was the real power. So in order for me to be effective with that group I had to reach both of these people. I had to reach the chief because I needed the official sanction, and I had to reach this other person because I needed to get the group mobilized. To get that approval I had to meet them on their own territory. In this particular situation the meeting with the chief was fairly brief and formal; the meeting with the heir apparent was informal, lasted much longer and involved a more personal assessing process.

In trying to mobilize a group to action there are several points that should be kept in mind. One is whether the needs of the people that might be involved in an issue can be met through their joining the group. The next is that you need to look at the power situation and determine who has what power, and how to influence the power channels that really made the decisions. How does one group's power shape up against that of the other groups, and what might you change about that? A third point would be how can you mobilize people to your side by conveying the issue in the manner that will appeal to them. It becomes a public relations issue as well. You have to set up the issues in an appropriate way. I am not advocating that you lie or be dishonest about it, but you have to frame the issue in a certain way so that it has appeal and meaning for the people involved.

One important point about community organizing is that it is best not to set up a long-term committee with general objectives but rather to organize around specific issues. It is possible to generate considerable energy in a community around specific issues but it is very difficult to generate long-term energy. And the real key is that the issue should reflect a need in the community that people are prepared to take action on. It is, of course, necessary that there be a good chance of success with the particular issue. Most peoples' experience with bureaucracy is that one person can't have much effect. So it is important that people actually have success experience and feel their potency. As well, there needs to be a common feeling within the group so that a cohesiveness begins to develop. If those factors occur then it is possible to go on from that first issue to a second and a third, and gradually mobilize people in the community. For instance, and this is a limited although related example, consider the student council of a high school or university. What typically happens is that they are dysfunctional and students are apathetic. The only time that this is different is when there is a significant issue. At this point people often get involved. They won't maintain that energy for very long and most student councils strategically make the mistake of, rather than operating on an issue basis, operating on the general belief that everyone should be interested in the student council's activities. Being issue-focused involves meeting the needs of the people. The basic question a community citizen asks is "What am I going to get out of this?" And if enough will be derived from it, then energy will be committed. We can't depend just on altruism. I think that we have to assume that there has to be some self-interest involved. If we make that assumption and can build on it, then we can be more effective in terms of doing community work.

I was involved in student council activities in high school and university. One of the things that we did was create issues. They were real issues in that they had foundations in fact, but we would work on building up those issues to mobilize support. One situation involved a government having an extremely low amount of money in student bursaries and scholarships. We took on this issue, did a detailed economic study, put together a 35-page monograph, went to the press and had press meetings and briefed the opposition to the government. The things we did which made a big difference were to go on radio and television and also to publish half a million newspapers. The basic theme was "It is not fair to those who don't have the money that they should be prevented from going to university." This theme was a very acceptable one at the time, although it may have less impact in today's economic climate. However, we were able to generate considerable support and have some impact.

Another point is that one of the important roles of a community consultant is to provide a link to resources that the group needs.[2] Often people in a community you are helping to mobilize don't know what resources exist, or in some cases they don't know how to get access to them. Simple examples are people who don't know where to get social security assistance, or legal aid, or medical attention. So the linking role can become very important.

The final point to note is that you often set up a group or organization to bring about community change. This group or organization is usually comprised of volunteers. One way a volunteer organization or group differs from others that we have dealt with up to now is that it is a completely voluntary situation and is very easy to leave. It is harder to disassociate oneself from a family, and it is harder to disassociate oneself from a job; it is very easy to disassociate oneself from a volunteer organization. So the whole issue of motivation, reward, support, development, and training becomes very, very important in voluntary organizations. The voluntary organizations that are most successful are the ones that do the best job of integrating the needs of the movement to the needs of the individuals within it.

NOTES

1. These three approaches borrow from the three models developed by Jack Rothman. For a comprehensive treatment see an article "Three models of community organization practice" by Jack Rothman in *Social Work Practice* (New York: Columbia University Press, 1968).

2. One of the best articles I have come across on the linkage issue is "Linkage problems and processes in laboratory education" by Ronald Lippitt in *The Laboratory Method of Changing and Learning*, K.D. Benne, L.P. Bradford, J.R. Gibb and R.O. Lippitt, eds. (Palo Alto: Science and Behavior Books, 1975).

QUESTIONS

1. Use the consultants' human systems assessment model (Figure 10:1) to assess a community with which you are most familiar. What aspects are most difficult to assess?
2. Are there other dimensions which should be considered? Modify the model to better suit the situation.
3. Assess yourself on the three styles of community intervention, both in terms of your skill level and degree of comfort.

ANNOTATED BIBLIOGRAPHY

Annual Review of Sociology
> An excellent way to keep up with the field; covers the field of sociology with some excellent articles containing change implications.

Kahn, A.J. *Theory and Practice of Social Planning.* New York: Russell Sage Foundation, 1969.
> A very comprehensive view of one approach to community change. Contains many points that can be integrated into other approaches.

Journal of the Community Development Society
> A journal that is exclusively devoted to this area. Quality of articles varies considerably but well worth reading.

Kramer, R.M. & Specht, H. *Readings in Community Organization Practice.* 2nd ed. Englewood Cliffs, N.J.: Prentice Hall, 1975.
> An excellent book of readings that covers the field in a thorough and comprehensive manner.

Perlman. R. & Gurin, A. *Community Organization and Social Planning.* New York: John Wiley & Sons, 1972.
> A textbook that provides an integrated view of the field and contains much value at both a theoretical and a practical level.

Ross, M. *Community Organization: Theory, Principles and Practice.* 2nd ed. New York: Harper & Row, 1967.
> One of the most significant early books in the field (1955) has been updated and is still an excellent reference.

Rothman, J. *Planning and Organizing for Social Change.* New York: Columbia University Press, 1974.
> One of the most useful books available to practitioners. Presents a synthesis of research on social change and draws conclusions for practice. A mammoth undertaking presented in a very clear and understandable format.

PART THREE

Part Three of this book contains only one chapter. It deals with the integration of the models and considers alternate levels of intervention.

CHAPTER ELEVEN

Toward an integration

Before moving into the subject of integration I would like to review the major points we have considered. We first developed an assessment model which included the systems level; a systems analysis (a system having input, output, throughput, a feedback system, a boundary, and existing in an environment); a developmental feature (attempting to determine the developmental stage of the system); eight general factors (including objectives, structure, roles, communication, power, reward system, time, and space); and, the client-consultant relationship.

We then developed a nine-part model showing how systems actually change. This model involves analyzing the situation; looking at the potential for change; developing outcome criteria; generating alternative solutions; making a decision; developing a plan; implementing the plan; evaluating the success of the plan; and, finally, determining that the reward system will continue to support the change.

This change model applies to all human systems. It doesn't necessarily mean that a given system will always go through those steps in that order. As well, the time sequence of going through this change model varies considerably depending on the level of system. In a counseling session with one person the consultant may, in fact, go through that change model or parts of it as many as thirty or forty times in the same session. So this is not just a static model that occurs over months and months; it will require varying degrees of time depending on the particular situation.

The third point we considered was that there are seven systems levels of which consultants need some awareness. These include the intrapersonal, or individual level; the interpersonal level, or the relationship between two people; the group level, which includes both families and work teams; the intergroup level, which is in many ways similar to the interpersonal level; the organizational level, which often consists of various groups in a hierarchical structure; the relationship between organizations, or the interorganizational level; and, finally, the community level.

It is the thesis of this book that a consultant should have some awareness of all these levels of change. It doesn't necessarily mean that you have to be an expert in them all and it doesn't necessarily mean that you are going to spend equal time doing them all. It doesn't even mean that you are directly involved in them all. However, in terms of assessing problems you will find that the most leverage or advantage or potency you can get is to choose the right level or levels of intervention.

There are two ways that we can try to think about the levels. One is in terms of the change target. The change target can be any of the seven human systems levels. Our ultimate objective may be to change an individual relationship, an organization, or any of the other human systems levels. The second way to consider human systems levels is in terms of the level of intervention. I think that the next point is one of the most significant in our coverage of changing human systems. The change target and the level of intervention may be similar or they may be different. Let me explain this point by considering Figure 11:1. The seven levels are listed as both targets of change across the top of the matrix and as levels of intervention along the side of the matrix. You can see that it is at least theoretically possible to bring about any one of these change targets through any one of these levels of intervention. This provides 49 (7 x 7) different combinations of levels of intervention and targets of change. Let us consider a couple of examples. For instance, an individual comes to see us about some problems (individual target of change), and we find that the major problems result from the individual's distortion of reality; then the most appropriate intervention may be to set up individual counseling sessions (individual level of intervention). On the other hand, if the individual (target of change) we are seeing is a child, and we determine from our assessment that the child's major problems are caused by being caught in the middle of a conflict between the parents, then the most appropriate level of intervention would more likely be interpersonal (meeting with the parents to work on their conflict) or group (meeting with the whole family to deal with the total system conflict).

A second example would be in terms of dealing with an organiza-

TARGET OF CHANGE

	INTRAPERSONAL	INTERPERSONAL	GROUP	INTERGROUP	ORGANIZATION	INTERORGANIZATION	COMMUNITY
INTRAPERSONAL							
INTERPERSONAL							
GROUP							
INTERGROUP							
ORGANIZATION							
INTERORGANIZATION							
COMMUNITY							

LEVEL OF INTERVENTION

FIGURE 11:1 Targets of change and levels of intervention

tion. If we are called in to help an organization function more effectively (organization target of change) then we must choose our level of intervention based upon our assessment. For instance, the level of intervention may be the organization (developing a new performance appraisal system); the group (increasing the effectiveness of the senior management team); or, the individual (working with the president in order to delegate more effectively), to mention but a few of the possibilities. All of these levels of intervention may be effective in helping the organization to function more effectively (organization target of change), and the choice of levels results from a thorough assessment of the critical factors causing and maintaining the problems we examine.

The reason we can intervene at levels other than the level of the target of change is that there is an interrelationship between subsystems, systems and the environment, and the activities of one level often have significant effects on another. An intervention we make at one level isn't just limited to that level, but often has a ripple effect on other levels. It is analogous to throwing a stone into a pond; the impact of the stone does not just effect the water where it lands, but has a ripple effect throughout the pond.

One of the points you may find is that in order to affect a certain change target you may work at several levels simultaneously. You may work with one member of the family and also with the family as a whole at the same time. Or you can work with an organization or community agency at the same time as well. So you may have multiple intervention points in order to change one change target. Sometimes, if you pick the right combination, you can get additional leverage through a synergy effect. For instance, if you have two good leverage points, they sometimes produce more than twice as much impact. Therefore, looking for multiple intervention points can often be useful.

The other factor that you may discover is that rather than choosing multiple intervention points you may choose successive intervention points at different levels. For instance, in the example of working with a family, initially you may decide to work on some family problems and you bring the family together. Subsequently, you discover that one of the members of the family is having particular problems that need to be dealt with separately, so you might decide at that point to shift into an intrapersonal intervention.

Therefore, you have options in terms of how you work. Traditionally most of the literature focuses on only one level of intervention.

It can be very prescriptive in terms of what you should and shouldn't do. For instance, some family therapy literature says that you should only work with the intact family. If everyone can't be there you shouldn't do family therapy. In terms of this model that absolute prescription doesn't make any sense, except perhaps if you had a situation where someone who was very powerful in that family system was excluded and had the power to sabotage the whole change process.

Another function that this model serves is to help you become more clear about what, in point of fact, you are trying to change. Often the literature will talk about the change target and get it confused with the intervention level. For instance, in the organizational change area most of the literature is really about group change. There is seldom an attempt to show how this intervention level (group) will lead to differences in the change target (organization). The literature often fails to make a distinction between those two separate aspects. The important thing is to know what your ultimate change target is and what the link is between the level at which you are working and the level you ultimately want to change. If you are aware of that, and you know what the links are, then it is possible to work at many different levels either simultaneously or successively. This will give you more power and more effectiveness than working in more limited traditional ways.

A particularly important implication of the fact that the target of change, and the level of intervention can be different, is that often the target of change can be impacted by combining an intrapersonal level of intervention with a level of intervention similar to the target of change. For instance, in helping a group to operate more effectively (group target of change) it may be appropriate to intervene at both the intrapersonal (helping group leader to learn skills of conducting effective meetings) and group (acting as a process consultant in clarifying objectives of group) levels. The reason for this is that problems in human systems often result from the interaction of the system itself and the designated leader of the system. The leaders of the systems often do not have adequate skills to properly manage the system. Therefore, teaching the appropriate leadership skills can often complement other levels of intervention. Examples would include: teaching parents parenting skills; teaching group leaders group meeting skills; teaching organization managers management skills; and, teaching community leaders community organizing skills. It should be noted that the highest probability of change exists where both the individual levels and larger group levels are dealt with in relation to each other. For instance, training managers in conjunction with organization improvement will have more impact than doing either alone (either sending managers away to be trained without also addressing organization systems problems or developing a new system (such as a performance appraisal system) without training individuals in the skills required to manage and utilize that system).

I would like to conclude by presenting examples of the forty-nine possible interactions between the levels of change intervention and targets of change. I will do so by presenting three distinct perspectives. First we will consider a counselor or psychotherapist whose targets of change tend to be the intrapersonal, interpersonal (marital relationship), and group (family) levels. Since, theoretically, seven levels of intervention could be used for each target of change, we will consider 21 (7 x 3) combinations from the perspective of a counselor.

Next we will consider 14 (7 x 2) possible combinations for intergroup and organizational change targets from the perspective of a management or organization consultant.

Finally, we deal with 14 (7 x 2) possible combinations for interorganization and community levels of change from the perspective of a community consultant.

The counseling perspective

Individual target of change

When an individual comes to see a counselor (for the sake of this example let us assume that the client is a married man who has two children and works in an organization) the tendency is to treat the problem from an intrapsychic perspective and spend extensive time dealing with how the individual feels about the situation and perhaps dealing with earlier experiences (for instance, childhood) that may be contributing to the problem. While I do not doubt that this focus has some benefit, I object to the fact that the individual's environment is often not fully explored. In particular, the individual in this example is the linking pin between two critical systems, the family and the organization. And we know from our assessment of the interrelationship between systems that the activities of one system have a high potential to affect other systems. There-fore, it is quite possible that there is a relationship between intra-personal issues (feeling anxious), family problems (fights with a spouse), and work problems (decreased performance). Unfortu-nately counselors often do not look for, or fail to recognize, these interrelationships, and therefore are often not as effective as they might otherwise be.

Let me progress through some of the possibilities for handling this situation, and then deal with an example from my practice per-taining to this type of situation.

When an individual comes to a counselor with a problem it is possible to intervene at the intrapersonal level (set up individual counseling sessions to deal with issues such as depression and anxi-ety); interpersonal level (most likely with the spouse, but also possi-bly with someone from the work situation, particularly the boss); group level (most likely with the family, but possibly with the work team); intergroup level (bringing two groups together such as the family and work team—while this intervention is theoretically possi-ble it would seldom occur); organization level (assisting the individ-ual to intervene, or intervening on the client's behalf, regarding issues such as working conditions or the reward system); interorgani-zation level (bringing the organizations together would probably not occur from this target of change); and, community (assisting the individual to intervene, or intervening on the client's behalf, on issues such as provision of family services). So we can see that when an individual comes to a counselor there are theoretically seven lev-els of intervention of which three are quite likely (intrapersonal, interpersonal, and group), two are possible (organization, commu-nity) and two are unlikely (intergroup, interorganization).

Let us first consider the two possible levels of intervention and then the three probable ones. Counselors tend not to intervene di-rectly or assist the client in intervening at the organization or com-munity levels even though these strategies may have important effects. Many problems have multiple causes and counselors often deal with one aspect without sufficient involvement in others. For instance, if someone complains of anxiety due to prejudice we may conclude that part of the problem is intrapersonal (some people can cope with prejudice more effectively and, therefore, likely have bet-ter coping mechanisms) and partly environmental (the environ-ment placing an unjust stress on an individual). Even though this makes sense, the tendency is still to ignore the environmental aspects and consider only the intrapersonal aspects. This may result in ineffective counseling.

I would like to give an example of a situation in which I was involved to further illustrate the options. I was called by a senior executive who was concerned about one of his senior staff. This person had recently shown significant changes in behavior, including lateness, irritability and incompletion of assignments. I agreed to meet, provided the individual was willing to do so.

When we met I began to explore the problems, and, in particular, the relationship between the individual's work situation and family situation. Clearly both were being affected by and contributing to this individual's problems. We decided to work together, and set up a plan whereby we would spend some time alone (to work on the intrapersonal aspects of the apparent depression); some time with this person's spouse and child, initially for assessment purposes and perhaps subsequently to provide marital and/or family therapy; and to meet with the boss, to assess the work situation, consider aspects that should be modified, and set up explicit contracts with regard to work performance expectations.

In the initial family session I tried to assess the relationships within the family, the role of the spouse in the present situation and, in particular, to determine any negative consequences on their child. On the basis of the interview and other data I had accumulated, I concluded that the child had not been negatively affected. Furthermore the spouse, although having experienced some stress from the present situation, was handling it well and was more skilled and sensitive than my client at an interpersonal level. Therefore, I scheduled some future sessions with them as a couple partially to work on problems in the relationship and partially to have one spouse assist the other with some interpersonal skill weaknesses.

In the initial session with the boss we got agreement on some of the presenting problems and clarified expectations. We then worked on some of the blocks (both personal and organizational) to effective performance and drew up some objectives for future performance.

Over a period of several months, through this tripartite approach, the initial problems lessened, although they certainly did not totally disappear. At an intrapersonal level my client felt more confident and alive. In terms of the family situation, this relationship improved with the participation of the spouse. In terms of the work situation, many organizational and personal blocks were lifted and work performance improved. The reason for this outcome, I believe, was that the major factors which were both causing and maintaining the problem were dealt with through a systematic interrelated approach.

Interpersonal target of change

For a counselor, the major interpersonal target of change is a marital relationship. Again, in dealing with this target of change several levels of intervention are possible. The most obvious of course is to see the couple together (interpersonal level). In fact, this is usually the most effective primary approach, and other approaches tend to supplement this one. The second level to consider is the intrapersonal level in which one or both of the spouses are seen alone. This can be useful at points when one person tends to be blocking the progress, or when relatively unrelated intrapersonal problems emerge in one of the partners. However, there is an inherent danger in seeing only one of the spouses in that this one will be labelled as the 'sick one.' Therefore, this potential problem must be weighed in any decision. A third option is to meet with the family of the couple, particularly in terms of their at-home children who may be affected by the conflict. At least it is often useful to conduct an initial family interview to assess potential problems and causes. Another type of group level intervention could be with the couples' parents or families of origin. This formation has some aspects of an intergroup level of intervention, although the interaction is so complex and the coalitions so changeable that it is difficult to determine which are the groups. As with the intrapersonal target of change the intergroup and interorganization interventions tend not to be used, and the organization and community interventions tend to be underutilized.

Group target of change

Counselors are also often involved with one type of group change, namely family therapy. This is an interesting situation in terms of the level of intervention, since often the problem is initially framed by the family as a problem of only one of its members. Therefore, often one of the first tasks is to define the problem in terms of the family. Especially initially, it is often a mistake to isolate an individual for treatment since that person will likely be ascribed the 'sick role.' However, clearly as well as the group (family) level of intervention, the counselor can intervene at an individual level. A third option is to intervene at an interpersonal level, particularly in terms of the parental relationship, but also in terms of a sibling relationship or the relationship between one of the parents and one of the children. In fact, during the course of family therapy the focus often shifts among the intrapersonal, the interpersonal, and the group levels. As with the other two targets of change (intrapersonal and interpersonal), there are seldom interventions at the intergroup and interorganization levels. However, there may be some interventions at either the organization level (particularly in terms of dealing with the school of the children) or the community level (particularly in terms of the services provided for the children).

The organization consultant perspective

While an organization consultant may at times deal with intrapersonal, interpersonal and group targets of change, we will not consider them since they have been covered previously.

Intergroup target of change

In terms of the intergroup target of change, the most obvious level of intervention is the intergroup level, in which we have members of each group together. The second most common intervention level is the interpersonal level in which representatives from each of the groups meet. It is also possible to intervene at the intrapersonal level (working with one or more of the individuals to develop skills); the group level (working to strengthen the cohesiveness, decision-making process or change perspective of a group); and the organization level (modifying organization policies, reward system or information system to put pressure on the two groups). It is unlikely that the interorganizational or community levels of intervention would be used (although it should be noted that if the groups were community-based rather than organization-based, pressure could be brought to bear on the groups from the community rather than from the organization).

Organization target of change

In terms of the organization target of change, the most obvious level of intervention would be the organization, in terms of areas such as policies, procedures, roles and information systems. In point of fact for the organization target of change, many interventions tend to be at other levels. For instance, at the intrapersonal level, one may help the company president to delegate more effectively; at the interpersonal level, one could help two senior staff members to amicably resolve their conflict; at the group level, one could assist the management team to conduct more effective meetings; at the intergroup level, one could help to resolve conflict between the production and sales departments.

The interorganizational and community levels of intervention can also be important when the target of change is an organization. Relations with other organizations including suppliers, clients, competitors and government regulatory agencies become critical. As well, relations with the community, particularly political and consumer groups, are becoming more and more important.

The community consultant perspective

While a community consultant may also have targets of change at the five previous levels (intrapersonal, interpersonal, group, intergroup, and organization) we will concentrate on the interorganization and community levels.

Interorganization target of change

The most obvious method of dealing with the interorganization change target is for an intervention at the interorganization level. In point of fact, except for fairly small organizations, the level of intervention is usually at the intergroup (representative teams from the organizations meet) or the interpersonal (representative individuals from the two organizations meet) levels. It is also possible to have the level of intervention at the intrapersonal level (trying to influence a key individual); at the group level (trying to influence a key group); at the organization level (trying to influence one of the organizations in terms of policy); or, the community level (bringing pressure to bear in terms of the reward or information systems).

Community target of change

When the target of change is the community, the most obvious level of intervention is the community itself in terms of its formal or informal structure, laws, policies, and rules. However, even when the target of change is the community, it is possible to operate at all six other levels as well. One may intervene at the intrapersonal level, in terms of influencing a key individual; at the interpersonal level, in terms of resolving a conflict between two key power figures; at the group level, in terms of developing a cohesive change group, which becomes the critical mass for the change process; at the intergroup level, in terms of conflicts between two gangs or two factions in the community; at the organization level, in terms of influencing the policy of key community businesses or social agencies; and at the interorganization level, in terms of developing the relationship between two non-cooperating organizations.

QUESTIONS

1. Assess your competence in each of the seven intervention levels.
2. Develop strategies to increase your knowledge and competence in the weaker areas.
3. Develop strategies to recognize problems at the various levels and ways of handling them yourself, building professional teams or making appropriate referrals.
4. Develop examples from your work or situations where the change target differed from the intervention target.
5. Develop examples from your work or situations where multiple (either simultaneous or successive) change targets were used.

INDEX